# To Show What an Indian Can Do

Sports at  Schools

## John Bloom

*Sport and Culture Series, Volume 2*

University of Minnesota Press
Minneapolis • London

MINNESOTA

An earlier version of chapter 2 appeared as "'There's Madness in the Air': Popular Representation of Indian Boarding School Sports and the 1926 Haskell Homecoming," in S. Elizabeth Bird, ed., *Dressing in Feathers: The Construction of the Indian in American Popular Culture* (Boulder, Colo.: Westview Press, 1996). Copyright 1996 by Westview Press, Inc. Reprinted by permission of Westview Press, a member of Perseus Books, L.L.C.

An earlier version of chapter 3 appeared as "'Show What an Indian Can Do': Sports, Memory, and Ethnic Identity at Federal Indian Boarding Schools," *Journal of American Indian Education* 35 (3) (spring 1996): 33–48. Used by permission. The *Journal of American Indian Education* is published by the Center for Indian Education, College of Education, Arizona State University, P.O. Box 871311, Tempe, AZ 85287-1311.

Published by the University of Minnesota Press
111 Third Avenue South, Suite 290
Minneapolis, MN 55401-2520
http://www.upress.umn.edu

Printed in the United States of America on acid-free paper

Library of Congress Cataloging-in-Publication Data

Bloom, John, 1962–
    To show what an Indian can do : sports at Native American boarding
schools / John Bloom.
        p. cm.—(Sport and culture series ; v. 2)
    Includes bibliographical references and index.
    ISBN 0-8166-3651-6 (hc : acid-free paper)—ISBN 0-8166-3652-4 (pb:
acid-free paper)
        1. Indians of North America—Sports. 2. Indians of North
America—Education. 3. Sports—United States—History. 4.
Off-reservation boarding schools—Unites States—History. 5.
Discrimination in sports—United States—History. 6. United
States—Race relations. 7. Unites States—Social conditions. I. Title.
II. Series.
    E98.G2  B56  2000
    796'.089'97—dc21

                                                    00-008865

The University of Minnesota is an equal-opportunity educator and employer.

11 10 09 08 07 06 05 04 03 02 01 00          10 9 8 7 6 5 4 3 2 1

# To Show What an Indian Can Do

**SPORT AND CULTURE SERIES**
**TOBY MILLER AND M. ANN HALL, EDITORS**

# Contents

# Acknowledgments

In writing this book, I owe a debt of gratitude to a great many who made it possible, who encouraged me in writing about this topic, and who accepted me into their homes and told me their stories. First and most important, I would like to acknowledge Narciso Abeyta, Stella Bahe, Janice Becenti, Alice Collins, Arnold Collins, Reginald DeFoe, Mike Gorospe, Jack Jones, George McCully, Kenneth Moore, Marvin Pulliser, Julia Renquist, Joe Sando, and John Wood, the narrators who allowed me to stick a microphone in front of their faces and who dared to let others hear their voices. I would like to especially thank Julia Renquist for her warm hospitality and for her work setting up a group interview at her own behest.

A number of foundations and institutions were also crucial to the research I conducted for this book. I was first able to delve into this topic while at a Summer Seminar for College Teachers on Native American history at the University of Arizona sponsored by the National Endowment for the Humanities (NEH). Such seminars have been extremely valuable for independent scholars such as myself, as well as for teachers at community colleges and small colleges. The NEH Summer Seminar program has allowed us to strengthen our backgrounds in important research topics and to produce original contributions to our disciplines. Without the program, this book would not exist, and I hope that it continues to fund topics, like Native American history, that critically reflect upon issues of social justice, imperialism, and power in the United States. I would like to thank the seminar director, Roger Nichols, along with participants David Beck, Michele Butts, George Castile, Guy Clermont, Tom Colbert, Diana George, George Lankevich, Laura Klein, Dan Mandell, Jim Pierson, Vera Reber, and John Snider for the lively debates they ignited and for their careful readings of my early work on boarding school sports.

I conducted the bulk of my research while on a year-long fellow-ship from the American Council of Learned Societies during the 1994/95 academic year. During that time I was able to travel to archives, libraries, and boarding schools to conduct oral histories and to carry out primary research. I would particularly like to thank the archivists at the National Archives and Records Administration in Ft. Worth, Texas; Kansas City, Missouri; and Washington, D.C., and at the Cumberland County His-torical Society in Carlisle, Pennsylvania; the Kansas Collection at the University of Kansas; and the Pipestone County Historical Society for their assistance. The administration and staff at the Ft. Wingate Indian School, Haskell Indian Nations University, and Santa Fe Indian School provided generous access to their campuses and their collections of photographs and documents. Oral history transcripts of the interview with Arthur Harris in chapter 5 come from the Doris Duke Oral History Collection at the Arizona State museum in Tucson. I would like to express my appreciation both to the Doris Duke Foundation and to the Arizona State Museum for allowing me to print these materials. I also thank Robert Euler for granting me permission to use this interview. In addi-tion, I have quoted from oral history interviews that are part of the Doris Duke collections at the University of Oklahoma and the University of New Mexico. Many of the oral history interviews from former Santa Fe Indian School students come from the First One Hundred Years Oral History Project, collected at the Santa Fe Indian School library. I would like to express my appreciation for being allowed to look at and quote from these collections.

A number of individuals have shared ideas and materials and pro-vided encouragement throughout this project. In particular, Liz Bird,

Brenda Child, and K. Tsianina Lomawaima provided comments on early articles that formed the foundation for this book, and they showed an interest and enthusiasm that helped me keep writing. Michael Willard and Joe Austin also provided important editorial comments for the chapter on boarding school boxing that they included in their book on youth culture in the United States. Lonna Malmsheimer shared important records with me on the Carlisle Indian School. I would like to express a special acknowledgment to Sally Hyer, who not only steered me toward several people to interview, allowed me to use photographs in her collection, and shared her own research on the Santa Fe Indian School but also provided invaluable support. Norm Yetman graciously housed me during my research visit to Lawrence. Amy Farrell, Wendy Kozol, and Sharon O'Brien all read early drafts and provided comments for revision.

I would also like to thank editor Jennifer Moore at the University of Minnesota Press, as well as the anonymous reader whose comments were extremely helpful in my revisions of this manuscript.

My parents, Maxine and Sidney Bloom, are a constant source of love, support, and newspaper clippings. Other family and friends have been at my side through crises that were not related to this book but accompanied my writing of it. I would particularly like to acknowledge Jim Bloom, Lois Farrell, Jim Farrell, Stuart Dean Graybill, George Lipsitz, Ann Midgley, Pat Midgley, and Sharon O'Brien. I would also like to thank the staff of the Dickinson College Children's Center, including Marcia Fraker, Jodi Goodling, and Sue Shank, for the care they provided for my daughter each week as I worked on this book.

My daughter, Catherine Ann Farrell Bloom, and my son, Nicholas Farrell Bloom, inspire me with their love, laughter, humor, questions, food fights, and patience in putting up with the obsessive mood swings that seem to accompany anything I am writing. Finally, my wife, Amy Farrell, gives me the strength to keep on hitting the keyboard, stares at me when I recount sports trivia, corrects my grammar and punctuation, and is my partner in love and life.

# Introduction

In October 1997 Grace Thorpe arrived in Carlisle, Pennsylvania, with a petition in her hand. Most often, when she is engaged in political activism of this nature, Thorpe is rallying to protect the environment from nuclear waste. But this time she was involved in a different cause. She had come to this central Pennsylvania town to collect signatures to endorse her father, the great Jim Thorpe, as the century's greatest athlete. Indeed, there have been few other athletes who have come close to accomplishing what Jim Thorpe was able to do in his athletic life: He won gold medals in the Amateur Athletic Union (AAU) and Olympic games for the decathlon and pentathlon; he had a distinguished professional baseball career; and he was a Hall of Fame professional football player. In fact, the Associated Press in 1950 named Thorpe the greatest athlete of the first half of the twentieth century. However, after fifty years of National Basketball Association (NBA) Finals and Super Bowls, *Wide World of Sports* broadcasts, and *ESPN Sportcenter*, few today know much about athletes who, like Thorpe, never made it under the Fox Sportscope. To Grace Thorpe, her father's achievements are too important to forget just because they did not take place on television: "I just personally think he was the greatest all-around athlete of the century and I just felt I can do something about that" (Miller and Wenner 1997).

Jim Thorpe's daughter chose to stop in Carlisle on her petition drive because Carlisle was one of the most important places in her father's life. It was here that he first achieved national recognition playing football and running track for the Carlisle Indian School, the first federally operated boarding school in the United States built to educate and assimilate Native Americans. For some, it may seem puzzling that a committed political activist would put this kind of effort into a sports poll, not to mention one in which her father probably stands little chance against the likes of Michael Jordan or even Deion Sanders. Yet her work on behalf of Jim Thorpe's legacy is a testimony to the significance of the history of sports at such boarding schools as Carlisle and among Native Americans. Mainstream sports, like football, were first introduced at boarding schools as part of a larger effort to erase Native American culture and history from memory. Ironically, however, they ended up being a source of pride for students and their children, a resource for pleasure, and an instrument through which they creatively constituted and reformulated their identities. The following pages explore this irony, one that reveals how sports uniquely constituted the cultural politics involved in federal efforts to educate Native Americans.

The federal government began its boarding school program for Native Americans during the late nineteenth century as part of a crusade by a coalition of reformers who aimed to assimilate Native Americans into dominant Anglo-Protestant society through education. With a fervor that was partly evangelical and partly militaristic, the creators of the boarding school system hoped that through education, they could bring about a mass cultural conversion by waging war upon Native American identities and cultural memories. At their peak at the end of the nineteenth century and during the first two decades of the twentieth century, the federal government operated twenty-five boarding schools located at sites off reservations. Even more pupils attended boarding schools that the government built on reservations, and other students attended similar institutions operated by missionaries throughout the West and Midwest. In 1899, 20,712 Native American pupils attended federally operated schools. When the Carlisle Indian School closed in 1918, that number had increased to 25,396 (Coleman 1993, 48–49). During this period, the age of students attending boarding school varied widely. Many were sent off to reservation schools at age five, for example, while adults in their late twenties and early thirties sometimes attended boarding school as well.

The architects of the federal boarding school system never mentioned sports in their earliest arguments for creating these institutions. By the 1950s, however, out of federal Indian boarding schools had come such world-famous athletes as Thorpe, nationally ranked football teams, regionally dominant girls' and boys' basketball teams, and highly rated boxing teams. Indeed, to this day many nonindigenous U.S. citizens know of nothing about boarding schools created for Native Americans except their achievements in sports. Athletic teams and recreation formed the basis for much of the popular culture that students experienced and created at the schools. This book explores the relationship between sports as a form of popular culture and the politics of assimilation that characterized boarding school life between 1879 and 1960. The point, however, is not to provide a narrative history of boarding school sports that only highlights great teams and great athletes. Such books already exist, and although they provide important information and credit the often overlooked achievements of Native American sports figures, they do not explore the meanings and histories the sports evoke, nor the ways that sports are experienced and understood within the context of daily life.[1] Instead, this book examines sports as a "polysemic" phenomenon—a cultural form that gives voice to a variety of historical perspectives, social contexts, and cultural interpretations. It provides a series of case studies that illustrate ways that students, mass media, school administrators, coaches, and federal officials used sports to construct identities, express emotions, and struggle over the meaning of Indian education.

Over the past twenty years, a growing number of historians and anthropologists have taken up the study of federally operated boarding schools for Native Americans, examining them in relation to issues of conquest, cultural hegemony, ethnic identity, and resistance.[2] Drawing upon a wide variety of sources, including oral history, government documents, diaries, letters, and photographs, this scholarship has illuminated the pain and violence inflicted upon Native American children through the boarding school system, the creative strategies students employed to survive and rebel while attending boarding school, and the general importance of boarding schools to Native American populations in the United States during the twentieth century. This book is indebted to this body of scholarship, for it has allowed me to examine a form of popular culture that was an integral part of the daily lives many students experienced. Sports provided a popular image of modern Native Americans that the promoters of the Indian boarding school system used to promote their cause. Athletic contests, such as football games and track meets, were public spectacles that showcased popular heroes and exhibited principles of Protestant discipline. Yet students often enjoyed boarding school sports as well, and not always in ways that Anglo politicians and school administrators had imagined. In fact, even among advocates of boarding school education and assimilation, sports generated heated controversies and evoked contradictory values and responses. When students expressed pride or mischievous pleasure through sports and when politicians and reformers fretted over the corruption involved in amateur athletics, they revealed larger cultural tensions that surrounded efforts to assimilate Native Americans into Anglo-Protestant, capitalist society.

The off-reservation boarding school system grew out of policy changes by the federal government toward Native Americans during the late nineteenth century. During this period, a number of reformers, politicians, and religious leaders began to propose alternatives to the policy of having the military violently remove Native Americans from nonreservation lands that had characterized federal policy during the nineteenth century. Instead, they proposed an assimilationist approach to removal. That is, rather than getting rid of Native Americans by physical force, entire tribes and nations might be blended into mainstream, Anglo-Protestant norms, transforming their values and identities to such an extent that in just a few generations, "American Indians" would cease to exist (Hoxie 1984).

The federal government began to isolate two areas in which to concentrate this effort: land use and the education of children. The U.S. Congress addressed the land issue by adopting severalty laws, such as the Dawes Act of 1887, which allotted tribal members individual parcels of land to farm and manage. Such laws were intended to promote the ideal of independent farming, the patriarchal nuclear family, and individual land tenure, ending the communal land ownership that existed on many reservations.

Boarding schools were the cornerstone of educational policy. Drawing upon a model set forth by missionaries throughout the nineteenth century, boarding schools would take students away from their homes and often from their tribes and provide a rigidly disciplined education. As historian Clyde Ellis points out, the early creators of the boarding school system, such as its architect Thomas Jefferson Morgan and Carlisle Indian School founder Richard Henry Pratt, were not only optimistic that the assimilation of Native American children could take place. They also saw their own optimism as symbolic of a benevolence they claimed to feel toward indigenous people. They believed themselves to be defenders of Native American humanity, forming organizations with names such as the "Friends of the Indian" and proclaiming that they were defending the "right" of Indians to become "civilized" (Ellis 1996, 11). When Pratt spoke of boarding schools, for example, he evoked the idea that such places afforded Native Americans a chance to stand on their own feet as independent citizens, freeing them from living as subordinates dependent on federal aid. Addressing the Board of Indian Commissioners in 1895, for example, Pratt said,

> To me the Indian question does not center in lands in severalty. It does not center in any other phases that have been discussed here. It is a question of individualizing, of getting the Indian to stand with us shoulder to shoulder, and to take care of himself, and not to be dependent upon a department whose particular quality is a perpetuation of itself. I feel that the Indian can be made just as capable of taking care of his individual affairs as the rest of us. (*Annual Report of the Board of Indian Commissioners* 1895, 43).

As Ellis points out, the political climate that ushered in boarding schools was not to last very long. By the turn of the century, a new crop of progressive reformers took command in Washington. They did not agree that Native Americans could be educated in the same manner as people with European genealogy. This trend is perhaps best exemplified by the *Uniform Course of Study* (*UCS*), drafted by Estelle Reel, superintendent of Indian Schools between 1898 and 1910 (Lomawaima 1996, 5–31). Unlike Pratt, Reel believed that Native Americans were racially inferior to people with a European background. Her statement in the *UCS* about physical education is but one example of this perspective: "In order to get the best out of life, it is necessary to look into the physical condition of pupils and give them the training that will counteract the influences of unfortunate heredity and strengthen the physique, in order that they may be able to bear the strain that competition in business and earning a living will impose" (Reel 1901, 196).

The contrast between Reel and Pratt shows that there was not a single ideology that guided the creation and management of boarding schools. Rather, it reveals that beneath the apparently seamless rhetoric of assimilation that characterized the late nineteenth century, reformers faced significant conflicts and contradictions. When I first began working on this topic, I was interested in how schools used sports as a tool to assimilate students and promote to the general public the idea of Native American education. In addition, I recognized that schools employed sports in ways that revealed the high degree of racism and ethnocentrism that guided federal policy toward Native Americans. However, as I learned about the conflicts that erupted among those who supported boarding schools, I began to think in ways that complicated many of my initial assumptions and that led me to explore sports as a more richly textured and dynamic cultural form.

I conducted my initial research on sports at federal boarding schools for Native Americans while preparing to teach a course on sports and American culture at Pennsylvania State University at Harrisburg. At first, I saw this as an interesting topic that would grab the attention of my students and through which I could teach about such issues as assimilation, ethnic identity, and race in the United States. As I delved into my research, however, I began to recognize that sports were an important aspect of boarding school history in and of themselves. Students who attended these institutions cared a great deal about sports, and policy makers and officials who created and ran these schools spent a great deal of time promoting, regulating, and worrying about the effects of athletics and physical education. Students, school officials, and politicians not only understood sports as representing struggles over ethnic identity on a symbolic level; they also invested valuable resources in sports, negotiating ethnicity and ethnic identity through athletics in important ways.

From a very early date in the history of the federal Indian boarding school program, physical education was a core part of the curriculum at many schools. Educators hoped that calisthenics could literally foster moral and intellectual progress by altering the body types of students. Just before the turn of the century, institutions like Carlisle and Haskell Institute in Lawrence, Kansas, began high-profile athletic programs. Each fielded football teams that competed successfully against the best college squads in the country, and they trained some of the greatest athletes of the early twentieth century, including Thorpe, Hall of Fame baseball pitcher Charles Albert "Chief" Bender, football star Jon Levi, and distance runner Louis Tewanima (Oxendine 1988). Other schools also competed successfully in sports such as track, girls' basketball, and lacrosse. Unlike physical education or recreation, these athletic programs were created to provide schools with a valuable source of public relations, providing "proof" that Native American children could be assimilated and taught to compete with grace and sportsmanship.

Sports, however, were not only an important part of the scheme that some had for blending indigenous cultures into the melting pot. Although the high-profile athletic programs at Carlisle and Haskell did not last, sports ended up becoming institutionalized into the very fabric of daily life at boarding schools and became a part of the culture that students created for themselves at these institutions. Alice Littlefield, in her oral history of students who attended the Mt. Pleasant Indian School in Michigan, argues that the historical position that American Indian students faced in boarding school made sports an important source of pride, one that ran counter to federal assimilationist ideologies. Littlefield found in her interviews that former students, particularly men, had vivid memories of Mt. Pleasant competing successfully on the high school level in football and basketball, and especially of times when they beat non-Indian opponents. "Given the assimilationist aims of the BIA educational system, athletic prowess became a symbol of Indian identity and Indian pride"(Littlefield 1989, 438).

Littlefield's conclusions suggest that sports played a complex role in boarding school life, one that posed specific possibilities for Native American students to creatively reimagine their cultural memories, traditions, and identities. At the same time, Littlefield's observations about sports being a site for expressions of resistance are unique, for they tend to conflict with what other scholars have observed about the relationship of school sports to youth and social reproduction. For example, cultural analysts like Stanley Aronowitz and Douglas Foley have also studied the more-than-century-long relationship of school-sponsored athletics to the cultural construction of youth in the United States. Their work has shown how athletic competition fosters conservative values and behavioral norms. In his exploration of contemporary working-class culture during the early 1970s, for example, Stanley Aronowitz argues that school operates as an institution of socialization for young people in capitalist societies and that officially sponsored sports are part of a process in which play becomes serious competition and in which more voluntary forms of recreation, like intramurals, "are denigrated"(Aronowitz 1973, 76). He argues that officially sponsored high school sports teams alienate most people from participation in the game, as the majority experience a high school game as passive spectators (62–67).

Like Aronowitz, Douglas Foley has carefully examined school sports as an important cultural form in which young people "learn capitalist culture." Foley examines a local high school football team as an ethnographer and interprets it as being engaged in a community ritual that ultimately reinforces patriarchal norms, race and class hierarchies, and militaristic values. By focusing on the event at that level, Foley exposes the limitations of sports as a vehicle for cultural resistance and instead reveals "the durability of the politically unprogressive cultural traditions that 'the people' find pleasurable and self-serving" (Foley 1990, 28–62; 200). Foley's research shows in detail how local businesses, Anglo community leaders, local boosters, and male citizens all invest heavily in making the football game a symbolic centerpiece of local life. As a cultural site for the expressions and emotions of young people, Foley understands sports as more of a rehearsal for prescribed adult roles than an imaginative vehicle through which alternatives are explored.

If, indeed, one acknowledges the conservative cultural codes and social functions that sports tend to provide, then how is it possible for Native American students to have expressed themselves in any but the most limiting ways through the athletic competition that took place at boarding schools? The oral histories that Littlefield conducted suggest that alternative ways of remembering and understanding sports are possible. Even though mainstream sports were intended to assimilate the native children and teenagers who attended boarding schools, former students expressed a type of ethnic pride in their memories of sports, a pride that conveyed antiassimilationist sentiments.

If one understands ethnicity as a constant process that, in the words of Michael Fischer, emerges out of struggle, such an irony is not necessarily something that we would want to explain away. April Schultz, in her work on ethnic identity and creation, has argued that cultural experiences that might on the surface seem to provide evidence of assimilation often, when examined more closely, convey a range of meanings, including some that run counter to dominant values and ideological perspectives. Schultz writes about Norwegian immigrant identity, focusing on the 1925 Norwegian-American Immigration Centennial. Most historians have interpreted this festival as a benchmark event, a ritual transformation of Norwegian-Americans into Americans. Yet Schultz understands it as a far more dynamic celebration, one that certainly celebrated a degree of assimilation, but one that also contained fragments of cultural memory that challenged dominant notions of national identity. Schultz concludes that ethnic identities are a "process of identification at a particular moment to cope with historical realities" rather than fixed items that are either maintained or lost (Schultz 1991, 1267). Ethnicity is a constant process in which historical and cultural memory is rendered meaningful in dialogue with the social and cultural contexts presented at any historical moment.

Such a dialogic approach to ethnic identity is particularly relevant to boarding school history, where students from multiple cultures and backgrounds intermingled and created complex identities and affiliations. In addition, it provides a useful model for understanding how Native Americans in the twentieth century have understood their identities within the cultural forms available to them. In the words of Patricia Albers and William James, who studied ethnic identity and creation among the Santee (Sioux), ethnicity is actually part of a dialectic process in which people "differentiate and label themselves in relation to others" within the "concrete circumstances and dynamics of social relationships" that are present at a moment in history and that help define how groups are differentiated from one another (Albers and James 1986, 12).

I have divided this book into five chapters. The first two explore the emergence of high-profile sports programs at Carlisle and the multilayered popular narratives that were created through the publicity that the Haskell Institute football team generated. Each chapter illustrates that sports helped to justify and promote the educational mission of boarding schools by displaying Native Americans behaving and even competing in a manner that was contained, civilized, and restrained. Yet such publicity also created controversy, for it contradicted these same goals by appealing to desires and passions that the public enjoyed in sports and popular culture and generally associated with Native Americans. These tensions reveal that sports were not employed with any coherent or seamless ideology but, rather, were a cultural form that could elicit a variety of interpretations even within dominant cultural contexts.

The final three chapters of the book explore how students were able to take advantage of this ideological incoherence and through sports experience pride, pleasure, and the creative formation of identity. Whereas the first two chapters focus more upon the conflicting ideas of school promoters, administrators, and the popular press, the last three chapters focus more upon the memories and ideas of students themselves. Chapter 5 addresses how sports are remembered in personal narratives created by boarding school graduates. Focusing upon a particularly engaging oral history, it illustrates how sports provide a critical point of reference for narratives about boarding school life and about Native American history.

As a non-Native academic scholar, boarding schools have not been a part of any history that I have experienced personally. In fact, I only really learned of their importance when I took an American Indian Studies course in graduate school at the University of Minnesota on urban Indians, taught by Ron Libertus. Beginning with that course, and continuing through my research on this topic, I learned how much my ethnic and racial identity have protected me from the negative consequences of government policies directed toward Native peoples and how my whiteness has also allowed me to materially benefit from the dispossession and disenfranchisement of American Indians. Yet because of this, I have also learned how much my own social position today is a result of historical events that link everyone in North America to its indigenous history.

Given the scope, magnitude, and effects of the federal effort to educate Native Americans between 1879 and the late 1960s, attention to student popular culture, sport, and leisure might seem somewhat trivial. Even many as critical of the boarding school system as I am might be tempted to discount such activities as little more than an "escape" from the realities of domination that defined these institutions. Yet given the effort by educators of Native Americans to structure and control leisure, play, and pleasure, it is at least worth asking what was at stake for students, teachers, and the federal government in the creativity, expression, and desire that students might reveal in the time they spent together unsupervised. Although administrators worked very hard to ensure that the activities of the students were strictly regimented, it would be a mistake to assume that their outcome was straightforward. Boarding school students clearly showed the capacity to take advantage of spaces wherever they could find them to play. When confined within the walls of an Indian boarding school, one must take advantage of any chance to escape.

# CHAPTER 1

# Native American
# Athletics and Assimilation

I have given the subject of football more thought this year than
in all the previous years, and am becoming convinced that good,
honest, fair, straight football is almost an impossibility.

—*Richard Henry Pratt, letter to Edward C. Mann, 1896*

Football players must be abstemious and moral in order to succeed.
If it was in my power to bring every Indian into the game of football,
to contend as my boys have contended with the different young men
of the colleges, I would do it, and feel that I was doing them an act
of the greatest Christian kindness, and elevating them from the hell of
their home life and reservation degradation into paradise.

—*Richard Henry Pratt, letter to Bishop McCabe, 1897*

Athletic contests, teams, and games existed at Indian boarding schools
on a level of symbolic activity that was no less important than the day-to-
day work and teaching that was done at these institutions. Politicians,
clergy, journalists, and boarding school administrators fiercely debated
their meaning and role in boarding school life. As the quotations from
Carlisle Indian School founder Richard Henry Pratt suggest, these
debates even took place within the minds of a single individual. Each
representation of sports reveals conflicts over racial ideology, assimilation, exploitation, violence, sexuality, and the meaning of success. At first
glance, sports at federal Indian boarding schools might seem to be one
more aspect of a curriculum designed to discipline minds and bodies, or
they might be seen as a public relations ploy meant to display the suc-
cesses of these institutions in their battle for the conquest of students'
souls and for patrons' political and financial support. Indeed, sports were

these things, but they did not do these jobs without stirring up controversy and raising troubling questions over and over again.

In his now-classic study of slavery and slave narratives, George
Rawick argues that Africans who came to America as slaves were beset
with a core contradiction. On the one hand, the institution of slavery
demanded of them that they relinquish all memory of their past in Africa.
On the other hand, however, African slaves could not do this, for the past
is something that is an integral part of any collective memory of a people
with common experiences, and it is something that is almost impossible
to erase. Rawick asks, "How was this contradiction between the denial of
the right and ability of the slave from Africa to act out the content of
his mind and memory and the fact that he had to do this resolved?"
(Rawick 1972, 8). For Rawick, the contradiction only became resolved in
the formation of an African American community and culture, where the
"victim" of slavery also became a "rebel in process." Only when this contradiction became too great for African slaves to stand did they become
rebels in action, but in the formation of an African American culture,
slaves developed the subjectivities, identities, and community formations
that would prepare them to act in their own behalf.

Boarding schools created by the federal government for Native
Americans at the turn of the century were not plantations, and students at
the schools might not always have been slaves. However, as with slavery,
these institutions demanded that Native Americans reject their histories
and identities and that students appropriate identities that served the
ideological interests that were consistent with their own subjugation. And
like those who came to America as slaves from Africa, Native Americans
could not erase their own past from their minds and memories. Students
who came to boarding schools created their own communities, identities,
and cultures out of the contradictions they confronted. Sports and popular culture provided a vital area in which they did so.

Given the scope of federal education policy aimed at Native Americans, it might seem unlikely that boarding school students could have
ever found room to develop a community within the confines of a boarding school. Superintendents and school administrators strictly enforced

rules, particularly during the first five decades after the institution of the boarding schools. During this period, students encountered a strict universal course of study, were forced to march in military drills and wear military uniforms, constantly confronted malnourishment and disease, and were physically beaten and cruelly humiliated for such infractions as speaking their native languages.

Yet even at their most oppressive, when student time was almost entirely occupied by chores, classes, marching, and discipline, the demands that boarding schools made upon students were never complete. Students found spaces, moments in time, and recreational activities in which to form their own alliances and communities, either through mischief, subversion of rules, or creation of their own identities and subcultures (Child 1993; Ellis 1996; Hyer 1990; Littlefield 1989; Lomawaima 1993 and 1994; McBeth 1984). In addition, even though the various goals of federal education policies toward Native Americans were often sweeping in their breadth, they changed over time, and in and of themselves they embodied contradictory points of view and perspectives. In other words, the demands that schools made upon students were not always consistent, and their inconsistencies reflect areas in which federal policy failed to achieve totality, where students could find room to create their own identities and act on their own behalf. Sports at Indian boarding schools dramatically embodied many of the contradictions that characterized the motives and ideologies of this federal effort to educate and assimilate Native Americans.

## Sports and Ideology at Carlisle

Most discussions of sports at federal Indian boarding schools begin with the Carlisle Indian School in Carlisle, Pennsylvania, at the turn of the century and end with the Haskell Institute in Lawrence, Kansas, during the 1920s. Although this book will expand this discussion to include many other boarding schools and time periods, it is important to recognize the central role that both played in establishing athletics as a fundamental part of boarding school life for Native Americans in the United States. Like other off-reservation boarding schools, Carlisle enrolled many students over the age of eighteen. Even though the school curriculum was at the elementary and secondary level, the age of the school's students allowed it to compete against the top collegiate teams of its era. It is at Carlisle that sports first became instituted in the federal Indian boarding schools on an interscholastic basis, where nationally and internationally famous athletes emerged in such sports as baseball, football, and track. In addition, particularly at Carlisle, the possibilities of using sports as a public relations tool, as well as the problems that came along with employing them this way, first came to fruition. At Carlisle, school leaders, particularly the school's founder, Richard Henry Pratt, discovered in sports a form of popular culture that was the most effective way to publicly represent an equation between success and the disciplined control over bodily passions.

It is probably not much of a coincidence that the Carlisle Indian School would be the most famous athletic program in the boarding school system. Although the late nineteenth century represented the first significant investment by the federal government in Native American education, schools never received adequate funding, and most faced severe financial hardships (Ellis 1996). Given these constraints, a school would need to have a superintendent particularly committed to the development of an athletic program. Richard Henry Pratt was just such a person. In a particularly prophetic passage in Carlisle's second annual report, Pratt wrote in regard to his plans to construct a boy's gymnasium, "Regular physical instruction is given, and from all that can now be seen we may eventually rival Cornell, Amherst, or Columbia in athletic prowess" (*Annual Report of the Commissioner of Indian Affairs* 1881, 247). This is a remarkable statement, given that Carlisle would not even field a football team of any kind until 1891, a full decade after Pratt wrote this comment.

Pratt must certainly have written this statement with some knowledge of the public relations possibilities of fielding a nationally renowned athletic team. Pratt's reference to Ivy League colleges in 1881 came at a time when such schools were first competing in intercollegiate sports (Oriard 1993). College football in particular was emerging as a source of entertainment that drew the attention of a newspaper-reading public and of eastern, college-educated men. Athletic teams, however, also provided a particular kind of public relations, one that I argue resonated in important ways with the mission of boarding schools and with the relationship among racial ideology, sexuality, and capitalist discipline.

## Discipline, Sexuality, and Education

In her history of the Chilocco Indian School in northern Oklahoma, K. Tsianina Lomawaima writes, "[F]ederal boarding schools did not train Indian youth for assimilation into the American melting pot, but trained them in the work discipline of the Protestant ethic, to accept their proper place in society as a marginal class" (Lomawaima 1994, 99). This emphasis on constituting within students an internalized work discipline was a core aspect of the boarding school system. It was formulated around fundamental premises and ideologies of race and sexuality. Lomawaima writes of this disciplinary focus being most forcefully executed in the "physical training" that students received at schools, mostly in the form of military marching and drills:

> The federal emphasis on physical training reflected racist conceptions of the intrinsic link between uncivilized minds and undeveloped bodies. The boarding school exemplified Foucault's assertion that in Western, industrial societies' systems of "corrective" detention, "It is always the body that is at issue—the body and its forces, their utility and their docility, their distribution and their submission." (Lomawaima 1993, 228; quoting Foucault 1979, 25)

Annual reports, letters, and other public documents and statements by the creators of the federal boarding school system strongly support Lomawaima's point. The emphasis of most early writings by boarding school promoters reflects less of a concern with the teaching of specific skills and more of a concern with teaching behavior appropriate for work in a capitalist environment: self-discipline, delayed gratification, suppression of desire, and rationality. Consistent with the Victorian ideology that, as Lomawaima notes, guided the rules and curriculum in boarding schools, educators separated women and men and took special care to "domesticate" women out of a fear that they were more wild and uncontrolled than men and were likely to lure their male counterparts back away from "civilization." In Pratt's 1881 statement in the *Annual Report of the Commissioner of Indian Affairs to the Department of the Interior*, he wrote:

> It is impossible to overestimate the importance of careful training for Indian girls, for with the Indians, as with all other peoples, the home influence is the prevailing one. . . . It is the women who cling most tenaciously to heathen rites and superstitions and perpetuate them by their instructions to the children. (*Annual Report of the Commissioner of Indian Affairs* 1881, 246–47)

Thus, female and male students at boarding schools were segregated from one another and rarely allowed to interact socially. This concern over gender was strongly intertwined with the racial ideology of boarding school promoters, who associated Native Americans in general with wild, uncontrolled passions and behaviors. In fact, part of the rationale for creating a boarding school system rather than a day school system was the fear that students would be lured away from "civilization" when they returned to their homes. Reporting on the opening of a boarding school in Benton County, Oregon, agent E. A. Swan of the Bureau of Indian Affairs (BIA) wrote in the 1881 annual report that the fifty new students (or in his words "favored inmates") "present a complete transformation from their wretched condition when received, many of them wild, filthy, illy clad, and indolent, going from their homes and returning at will. Now they exhibit marked advancement in deportment, industry, and taste" (*Annual Report of the Commissioner of Indian Affairs* 1881, 206).

In the 1883 *Annual Report*, Carlisle's school physician O. G. Given attributed the six deaths due to illness among students the previous year to racial characteristics that he linked with sexuality. First he included his assessment of tuberculosis, a disease that had become a deadly epidemic among students at Carlisle, within a discussion of venereal disease. Then he speculated as to why tuberculosis and venereal disease were common and deadly among Native American students. He wrote, "The opinion generally prevails that Indians as a race are physically strong. In regard to this I would say that where so much immorality and lewdness exists as does among the Indians there must of necessity be a great deal of venereal disease" (*Annual Report of the Commissioner of Indian Affairs* 1883, 164–65). Given's solution to this problem was to promote vocational training so that students would learn "civilized industry" and "character." These factors, along with a proper diet and "regular physical exercise," he argued, would enhance student chances of "overcoming any hereditary weaknesses" (165).

Many who study the history of the federal boarding school system have noted that the early years were marked by a strong, assimilationist perspective, one in which administrators and the BIA understood Native Americans as fundamentally equal but culturally inferior human beings. Such scholarship tends to locate a more overtly racist set of policies emerging with the administration of Estelle Reel in 1898 (Ellis 1996; Ryan 1962). Indeed, it is true that Reel significantly changed policy in ways that reflected her belief in the biological inferiority of Native Americans when compared to people of northern-European descent. However, the statements by early supporters of federal Indian boarding schools reveal ways that their mission was also deeply guided by a racial discourse.

Rawick, drawing from the work of British historian E. P. Thompson, makes a connection between the subjective demands of capitalist work discipline and the development of a racial ideology in Europe during the Enlightenment and the Industrial Revolution. Rawick notes how a new capitalist work ethic required entirely new ways of looking at humanity, society, and the individual, one in which contractual relations replaced organic ones, the authority of the state expanded, and the market and the state superseded local or regional custom. Capitalist work required the separation of labor from other aspects of life, the rationalization and commodification of work, and the repression of "nonrational" desires. Rawick, however, argues that collective memories of previous social arrangements did not simply fade away. Instead, he writes, they lived on, but many old habits and rituals became understood as sinful, harmful, and unvirtuous. Racism, he asserts, is the product of this repressive process, for as northern Europeans, particularly the English, came into contact with Africans and Native Americans, they found a shadow of their precapitalist selves. Racism, in other words, developed out of an encounter not with differences that Europeans could not understand but with repressed desires that they understood too well but could not stand (Rawick 1972, 127–33).

David Roediger notes that during the nineteenth century, "'[c]ivilization' continued to define itself as a negation of 'savagery'—indeed, to invent savagery in order to define itself. 'White' attitudes toward manliness, land use, sexuality, individualism and violence were influenced by real contacts with, and fanciful ideas about, Native Americans" (1991, 21). The "civilizing" mission of boarding schools, their focus on internalized discipline and work ethic, reflects this very theme. Although he writes that working-class resentment toward Native Americans was qualitatively different from and far less severe than that expressed toward African Americans, he, like Rawick, notes the relationship between the repression inherent in wage labor and the transporting of repressed desire upon the racial "other." The texts created by those who supported boarding schools (reformers, military leaders, religious leaders, business leaders, etc.) represent the grinding poverty of Native American life and the alternative ways of living posed within their cultures as inconsistent with the progressive, utopian ideologies associated with capitalism during that era. Thus, justifications for boarding schools often contained vivid descriptions of grinding poverty while simultaneously referring to lurid images of sexual and bodily freedom. If Roediger and Rawick are correct, beneath the surface of such reports is an ambivalence, a repressed desire, even a nostalgia for what boarding schools themselves were attempting to displace.

As a source of public relations, sports provided more than just entertainment and name recognition. To someone like Pratt, they also offered a vivid opportunity to illustrate racial transformation. They publicly demonstrated controlled violence and physical competition, rationally coordinated bodily movement, and a corporate hierarchy of human organization. During the late nineteenth century, men's athletics, particularly football, provided a powerful way to publicly represent discipline and control through exhibitions of "manliness" and "sportsmanship." Yet they did not do so unproblematically.

Even when it began to offer sports and physical education to students, the Carlisle Indian School provided both females and males with opportunities to participate in recreation. However, like most other educational institutions of the time, the high-profile interscholastic sports, such as baseball and football, were for men only. Football in particular vividly demonstrated the dominant masculine ideology of this era: It was a game in which men could compete violently yet could still demonstrate gentlemanly sportsmanship and valor. For both fans and players, football evoked animalistic aggression. Yet a large part of its ideological power lay in the way that it rewarded the ability to rationally channel and control this same violent passion.

Football and other sports, however, ended up creating problems at Indian boarding schools even as they provided a source of public display consistent with the boarding school mission. In fact, what is most remarkable and consistent about the ways that boarding schools used sports is not necessarily the exploitation of the athletes (although athletes and nonathletes were certainly exploited) but, rather, the ambivalence of those who operated the institutions that would supposedly benefit from such exploitation. In the remainder of this chapter I will read two perspectives that exemplify some of the tensions that sports at Carlisle evoked. The first appears in letters and statements of Richard Henry Pratt with regard to football, and athletics more generally, at Carlisle. The second is evident in a set of articles that former Carlisle coach Glenn S. "Pop" Warner wrote for *Collier's Weekly* magazine during the 1930s. Throughout, I will examine the ambivalence that religious leaders, politicians, and boarding school administrators expressed about sports as a vehicle for expressing and displaying discipline, race, and sexuality.

## Richard Henry Pratt and Football

To Richard Henry Pratt, the Carlisle Indian School was a grand experiment in which he proposed to take Native American children and transform them into "imitation white men." His theories of Indian education were formulated while he was a lieutenant in the U.S. Cavalry and was assigned to take a group of Cheyenne prisoners of war to Ft. Marion (formerly the Castillo de San Marcos) in St. Augustine, Florida. While at the fort, Pratt set up a school for the inmates at which they were taught to read and write English, were converted to Christianity, and were eventually released. Some of them were "model citizens" who never returned to Cheyenne territory. Pratt proposed to set up a permanent school for Indian children in 1878, first at the Hampton Normal and Agricultural Institute in Virginia, an institution that had been established for African American descendants of slaves. A year later Pratt was able to secure space to create his own school at Carlisle, an abandoned military outpost in south-central Pennsylvania (Witmer 1993).

From 1881, when Pratt first requested funds to build a gymnasium, physical education and sports were a part of the curricular life he envisioned creating at the school. As much as this was meant to benefit the physical health and recreational needs of students, it was also a source of public display. In the first few years after Carlisle was opened, students would travel to local fairs and festivals to perform physical drills or play games for public audiences. These exhibitions resembled the famous before-and-after photographs that local photographer John Nicholas Choate took for the school. These photographs were meant to show the dramatic transformation that a Carlisle education made in students, transforming them from primitive natives to members of Western civilization. In the school's first annual report in 1880, for example, the committee of the Cumberland County Fair reported on an exhibit by the Carlisle Indian School:

> A case of Indian clothing, implements, ornaments, and curiosities attracted a very general attention, and, by the thoughtful, could not but be contrasted with the articles manufactured by the children at the school. There was seen

a suit dressed with scalps of the owner's Indian enemies and a female's sack ornamented with elk teeth; near them plain and neat clothing made by the apprentice tailors and seamstresses of the school. Moccasins trimmed with beads, in contrast with shoes made by the Indian pupils ... Rude and grotesque paintings side by side with very fine specimens of penmanship and plain drawing, showing what rapid progress the boys and girls have made.... A number of Indian boys afforded the crowds and visitors much entertainment by their exhibitions of pony riding, foot racing, and shooting with bow and arrow. (*Annual Report of the Commissioner of Indian Affairs* 1880, 181)

This was clearly a carefully designed display of the "progressive" work being done at the Carlisle Indian school. A few portions of it stand out, however, as revealing alternative interpretations of the event. The writer of the report notes that the message of progress being promoted could be discerned "by the thoughtful," yet the Native American "curiosities" attracted "very general attention." This raises the obvious question of whether such a "general" audience was "thoughtful" enough to read the event in the manner that school officials preferred. "Crowds of visitors" were entertained by the sports that the young male students brought with them to Carlisle. The Native American arts and crafts may have been "rude and grotesque" to the author of this report, but they also were what drew interest and excitement.

In 1882 students from the Carlisle Indian School participated in the second annual Exhibition of Progress in Philadelphia, at which boys and girls played games with children from the Friends' school. Among the games played by the boys was football, a game that would come to symbolize progress at Carlisle like no other, but that would also, from the beginning, evoke ambivalent feelings. By the early 1890s male students had begun organizing football games themselves, and they participated in informal scrimmages with nearby Dickinson College. In 1893 Carlisle organized a team, coached by a boys' disciplinarian named W. G. Thompson, to play a two-game schedule. By 1896 the school had begun playing a regular college-level schedule, and in 1899 it hired legendary coach Glenn S. "Pop" Warner (Witmer 1993, 43–47).

During these years, Carlisle's football team gained national recognition and fame. Early on, however, Pratt openly wavered in his opinion of the game, at times praising it as a vehicle to foment "progress" and at other times expressing dismay at its ugliness and violence. He wrote in his famous autobiography, *Battlefield and Classroom*, that he was first opposed to allowing students to play football because of the dangers it posed:

> Not having had experience with football and finding here and there a victim of accidental or intended violence, I was not especially pleased to encourage it. One day, Stacy Matlock, a Pawnee, one of our largest and finest young men, a foremost player, while playing with Dickinson on their field, had his leg broken below the knee and was brought in great agony to the school in a carriage. I had not gone to the game but went down to the hospital, helped to lift him from the carriage to the operating table, and stood by to aid in setting the bone. This produced such a revulsion against the game that I said, "This ends outside football for us," and had outside football dropped from the school's repertoire. (Pratt 1964, 316)

There is evidence that Pratt's concern over football's violence, as expressed in his autobiography, was sincere. Also in 1891, Pratt wrote to George Nukochluk of Unalaska, Alaska,

> Some of the boys are very much interested in football. The ground behind the school house, up to the fence adjoining the guard-house, is given them for a play-ground. They have been grading it and getting it in shape for some time.... The smaller boys have "shinny" [a ball game popular among many Native American groups] as their game for all hours, and though not so dangerous as football, in the accidents they get, yet a good many get bumps and black eyes in consequence. (Pratt Papers)

Although he does not here mention banning football, he does compare it unfavorably with a Native American sport that he notes is also violent. Indeed, because forward passing was against the earliest rules of football created by Walter Camp during the late nineteenth century, "mass plays" like the flying wedge were common in the sport, which made it an extremely violent game, arguably as violent as today's. Yet Pratt's expressed concern with violence in his autobiography, indeed, his vivid description of it, also lends legitimacy to his eventual endorsement of football. Throughout many of his writings about the game, he portrays himself as a reluctant convert to football. This early stance would serve him well in the future, helping him emphasize his rational interest in the game, an interest he defensively expressed both publicly and privately. In 1896, for example, when the Carlisle football team first began to achieve national notoriety and to win games against well-respected opponents, Pratt began to express in letters some enthusiasm for football. Yet his enthusiasm was always tempered by a defensive posture in which he struggled to assert that football was a worthwhile pursuit for Carlisle students. In fact, at times he even repeated his earlier concerns over the game. For example, he wrote to Edward C. Mann on December 4, 1896, "I have given the subject of football more thought this year than in all the previous years, and am becoming convinced that good, honest, fair, straight football is almost an impossibility" (Pratt Papers).

Within the violence and intense combative emotion of the game, however, he argued that there lay the possibility to demonstrate how controlled he had taught his Native American students to become, how successful Carlisle had been at "taming" the wild children that came to its door. Throughout Pratt's writing about football, he emphasized sportsmanship, sometimes even more than winning. In a now-legendary story, Pratt wrote in his autobiography that the year after he had banned football, he was met by forty students demanding that the game be reinstated. After telling of his amusement at the students' eloquent arguments for allowing them to play, Pratt wrote that he was forced to "release my pent-up laughter" and "surrender" under two conditions:

> First, that you will never, under any circumstances, slug. That you will play fair straight through, and if the other fellows slug you will in no case return it. Can't you see that if you slug, people who are looking on will say, "There, that's the Indian of it. Just see them. They are savages and you can't get it

out of them." Our white fellows may do a lot of slugging and it causes little or no remark, but you have to make a record for your race. If the other fellows slug and you do not return it, very soon you will be the most famous football team in the country. If you can set an example of that kind for the white race, you will do a work in the highest interests of your people. (Pratt 1964, 317–18)

Illustrating the importance that he placed upon sportsmanship, Pratt's *second* condition, at least as he reports it in his memoir, is that the team commit itself to beating the "biggest football team in the country" in just "two, three, or four years" (318). Together, however, the ability to play "clean" and to win would provide Pratt with evidence that he was instilling in his male students "manly" character. In a letter to Abram R. Vail dated December 2, 1897, Pratt's concern with the violence of football had clearly subsided, as he argued that football injuries were often exaggerated in the press and that "not all those reported as killed by foot-ball are by any means." He goes on to argue for the virtues of football by writing that it helps develop masculine character traits:

> I have conferred with some of the best educators of the country, men whose opinions are taken as guides, and it is settled in their minds that proper foot-ball is one of the most manly sports ever invented for young men. My boys who play foot-ball are among the gentlest and best behaved in the school, and they have been made strong and exceedingly quick and active, and able to cope with difficulties; whereas those who take no part in foot-ball, who stand around with their hands in their pockets, become effeminate, and give no promise of aroused energy to meet the issues of life. Football players must be abstemious and moral in order to succeed. If it was in my power to bring every Indian into the game of foot-ball, to contend as my boys have contended with the different young men of the colleges, I would do it, and feel that I was doing them an act of the greatest Christian kindness, and elevating them from the hell of their home life and reservation degradation into paradise. (Pratt Papers)

Pratt in this letter echoes a theme that he reported having expressed to a different man of the cloth, one who had looked scornfully at the game of football at Carlisle. Testifying before the fourteenth annual Mohonk Conference of the Friends of the Indian, Pratt told the following anecdote:

> The other day a preacher came to see my football boys practice, and a friend of mine heard him talking about the Indian school afterwards, and he said, "If the Government of the United States has nothing better for the Indians to do than to play football, I am going to quit taking up collections in my church for Indian missionary work." If, through football, Indian boys can kick themselves into association and competition with white people, I would give every one a football. (*Annual Report of Board of Indian Commissioners* 1896, 49)

In these passages, Pratt ends up approving of football because, he argued, it instilled a competitive spirit in "Indian boys." Just as important, however, is his contention that the game turned these boys into men, that it both symbolically and literally served as a vehicle to transmit masculine character traits to young Native American males. During this era, an emerging stratum of middle-class, college-educated white men began expressing a symbolic, corporate masculinity by participating in football or by watching it as fans. Words like "gentleman" and "sportsman" permeated the vocabulary of those who wrote about the game, defining a masculine ideal around not only the ability to win violent battles but also the ability to control one's passions and behaviors.

The emphasis upon manliness is not only important because of the masculine ideals communicated through football; it is also important because of the issues of sexuality associated with Native Americans. School superintendents often portrayed Native American men as untrustworthy, irresponsible, lazy, and sexually free. In a word, boarding school promoters saw Native American men as unmanly. When Pratt wrote or spoke positively of football, he portrayed it as allowing Indian boys to perform with a masculine dignity, grace, and control that, according to his think-ing, they did not learn within their own civilizations. In his memoir of life at Carlisle, for example, he wrote of the following incident in which he was able to convey such a lesson to the football team during a close game with Yale, at that time the top college football team in the United States:

> During the progress of the game, one of our strong players carried the ball behind the goal for a touchdown. The umpire was a former Yale champion. He disallowed the touchdown. Our team was so indignant they started to leave the field.... I saw the disaster impending, ran across the field, and stopped them. I told them it would not do. "You must fight the battle out; if you leave you will be called quitters and probably lose us future opportu-nities." I said: "Listen, can't you hear that the crowd is with you? Now go back and play the game out and don't quit for any reason whatever." They all started back except the player who had made the touchdown. He was very indignant, saying, "Captain, that was as fair a touchdown as was ever made, and it belongs to us." I said: "Jakey, it is ours. The umpire's decision will not take it from us. Go back and do your best and wait for tomorrow morning's papers, and you will find that you are a bigger man because the touchdown was denied than you would be if it had been allowed. Now go and help the boys keep Carlisle at the top." He said, "All right, Captain," and went back and the game was renewed, much to the delight of the vast audience. That decision was all that gave Yale the game, but the papers were for us. (Pratt 1964, 319–20)

This story is a key part of the narrative that Pratt wrote about the football team in his memoir, and it is centered around his teaching one of "the boys" to be a "bigger man" than his opponent. Issues of sexuality and race are at the ideological core of this morality tale, for, as he claimed to have admonished his first students interested in football, any display of anger would only confirm to audiences that "they are savages." An unjust call was not really a problem for Pratt; rather, it was more an opportunity to show the extent to which his students could control their tempers and swallow their "Indian" pride, to vividly illustrate the degree to which they could repress their desires to express anger or take revenge and accept the rules of play that were handed to them.

Even though Pratt expressed in most of his public writings moral certainty and a love for the character-building qualities of football, many of his private letters reveal a different, conflicting side of his affection for the game. They show more concern with winning and a willingness to bend principles in order to create a more competitive team. Pratt's public writings and those of his private letters in which he defends football portray his interest in the game as a rational one, as emanating from his sincere mission to uplift the Indian race to the highest levels of civilization. Yet some of his private letters show more interest in winning games than in proving a point. For example, Pratt stated in numerous letters and public statements that the students who played football at Carlisle did not come to play sports. They were, instead, simply students, drawn from those enrolled, who happened to be interested in learning the game of football. In private letters, however, he zealously recruited football players who offered his team a hope of winning. In 1901, for example, Pratt wrote to W. R. Gulick,

> Since you were here, I learn from Mr. Walters, that you stated that there was a ponderous Indian, who would make a good foot ball man, who wanted to come to Carlisle. Have you such a one or two or three that weigh 180 up? We have some big battles to fight this Fall and I shall be glad to have them here to help us out, and would place transportation at once. (Pratt Papers)

This letter catches Pratt in a moment of hypocrisy. But perhaps more important, it highlights Pratt's deep interest in the football team, an interest that appears deeper than any aspiration to demonstrate clean play and sportsmanship. Pratt's public writings reflect the amateur ideal common among the sporting elite of the late nineteenth and early twentieth centuries, an ideal that distanced the supposedly "pure" sport of "gentlemen" from the vulgar, often professional, athletic contests of urban athletic clubs, semiprofessional leagues, and factory teams. His affirmation of such ideals was necessary and consistent with the strong, emotional paternalism he held toward students at Carlisle and toward Native Americans in general. Yet his paternalism also appears very similar to that of the slave masters, described by George Rawick, who distanced themselves from the vulgarity they associated with slaves of African descent while at the same time reveling in their contact with and power over those whom they held as chattel. Desires and fantasies teem just beneath the surface of the rationalist discourse that Pratt uses to defend the legitimacy of fielding a nationally recognized football team. A focus only on the tangible benefits, either financial or political, that sports brought to Carlisle misses the degree to which such publicity was one side of a coin whose other side was the spectacle of football—of the violent, vicarious, forbidden thrills to be had watching his Indian "boys."

This aspect of the early decades of Native American boarding school sports is a crucial one, for it extends beyond the mind-set of Richard Henry Pratt. It reflects larger cultural issues at the heart of the effort to assimilate Native Americans through boarding schools, and it reveals a level of ambivalence toward assimilation itself that may help us understand how athletics might have become a meaningful aspect of boarding school life for students. Articles and representations in the popular press provide a good place to "read" some of the dominant cultural motifs associated with boarding school athletics, as well as the contradictory ideas about race, sexuality, and desire that they embodied.

## "Pop" Warner's Public Memoirs of Carlisle

In October 1931 Glenn S. "Pop" Warner wrote a series of articles for *Collier's Weekly* magazine in which he recalled his years coaching at the Carlisle Indian School. The *Collier's* pieces reveal a great number of sometimes-conflicting sides to Warner: his occasionally overt racism, his grudging respect for the oppression felt by Native Americans, his paternalism, and his exploitative use of Native American customs. Yet they also provide a valuable illustration of the popular ideas that the Carlisle Indian School generated through its football team and the cultural contradictions that were generated by popular representations of Carlisle athletics.

Warner was hired to coach at Carlisle in 1899, and he stayed until

1914, with a brief hiatus between 1904 and 1906. At the school, he built the football program into a national power, and he also developed the men's athletic program in general. After he left Carlisle, he went on to further success at such major universities as Pittsburgh and Stanford. In the second part of the three-part series in *Collier's*, Warner wrote about the football teams that he had coached at Carlisle—teams that included such legendary players as Jim Thorpe, Gus Welch, and Lone Star Dietz— and that played the best teams in college football at the time, including Harvard, Army, and the ultimate powerhouse team, Yale. Speculating as to why his teams were so successful, Warner wrote,

> Carlisle had no traditions, but what the Indians did have was a very real race pride and a fierce determination to show the palefaces what they could do when the odds were even. It was not that they felt any definite bitterness against the conquering white, or against the government for years of unfair treatment, but rather they believed the armed contests between red men and white had never been waged on equal terms. . . . "You outnumbered us, and you also had the press agents," a young Sioux once said to me, "when the white man won it was always a battle. When we won it was a massacre." (Warner 1931a, 7)

This passage strikes a tone that is echoed consistently throughout the series of articles. In it, Warner uses stereotypical terms and images, as in his statement that the students at Carlisle liked to beat the "palefaces." Yet he also expresses a sympathy for Native Americans as victims of conquest who worked hard to set the record straight when given the opportunity to compete on an even playing field. Of course, the understanding that Warner seems to display in this quotation affirms that he was a moral and compassionate paternal leader of his Native American players, a presumption that is not necessarily born out in the historical record. Yet it is still significant that in order to position himself rhetorically as the Indians' "Pop," he seems to have felt it necessary to acknowledge a history of brutal military subjugation and force, even noting the discursive power of the victors to define history. A passage such as this, which appeared thirteen years after the Carlisle Indian School closed its doors, raises questions about the extent to which football at the school accomplished what Pratt had hoped it would. Instead of helping to incorporate indigenous peoples into a fictive national unity, it seems to have symbolized ways that Native Americans were defined by a national unity that through its very definition, systematically and symbolically excluded and subjugated them. Indeed, in Warner's writing, it is actually the marginal status of the Indian School teams that he recalled as having given them energy and as having provoked national interest.

Press coverage and popular images of the Carlisle Indian School football teams have provided a fascinating set of texts for the analysis of racism and Native American identity. Michael Oriard and Ward Churchill, Norbert Hill, and Mary Jo Barlow are among those who have analyzed them critically. Oriard's interpretation of popular writing about Native Americans tends to highlight the conflicting dominant cultural narratives embodied in sportswriting of the late nineteenth and early twentieth centuries, whereas Churchill, Hill, and Barlow tend to understand such representations as seamless examples of dominant racist motifs. The two perspectives provide an instructive dialogue for interpreting media images of Native American athletes, such as those created by Warner.

Oriard's book *Reading Football* is an analysis of the multiple cultural narratives that ran through football sportswriting of the late nineteenth century. He argues that no single set of allegorical meanings can be attributed to a sport like football; instead, one needs to examine the competing values and ideals that intersect at any particular historical moment when an athletic game might have been widely experienced and interpreted. In a section devoted to coverage of the Carlisle Indian School football team, Oriard writes that narratives of racial conquest and manifest destiny sit just beneath the surface of the journalistic prose that football fans read at the time. "In the daily press, Carlisle and its opponents became the redskins versus the palefaces in a series of narratives whose extravagance was bound only by the limits of the writers' imaginations" (Oriard 1993, 238). Oriard notes that the most overtly racist articles were by writers appearing in weekly magazines, particularly Caspar Whitney, who wrote football columns for *Harper's Weekly* and *Outing*. Oriard cites an especially vivid example of such racism in an article for *Harper's* by Jesse Lynch Williams, an article that he argues expressed an ethic of conquest and subjection of Native Americans. The article notes the sportsmanship that Pratt had hoped Carlisle would display, relating an anecdote about a Carlisle player who, after being knocked down in the open field by a Harvard defender, said to his opponent, "good tackle":

> In Williams's anecdote, the Carlisle ballcarrier represented his race as a model sportsman, but more: an honorable, uncomplaining, and wholly reconciled loser in a fair fight, the overt stake a football game but the implicit one a continent. In a stroke, through a simple but powerful narrative of sportsmanship, white Americans' manifest destiny was affirmed, its attendant guilt toward the land's displaced aborigines absolved. For Jesse Lynch Williams, as for Caspar Whitney, Theodore Roosevelt, and numerous others of their class and race, that narrative of fair play and racial destiny was a necessary fiction. (Oriard 1993, 247)

Oriard illustrates how the positive image created by exhibiting good sportsmanship could have a dark underside of subordination for Native Americans. Yet he also argues that such accounts do not represent the entire spectrum of writing about the Carlisle Indian School and that they differed in important ways from the writing one found in most daily newspapers. Oriard asserts that, like the weekly coverage of Carlisle, daily press accounts of games were racist. However, in addition to ideas of biological inferiority, they also embodied far more benign ideas about race:

> The racism in these accounts remained more implicit than open, the sort of racism found on the minstrel stage rather than in the pseudoscientific racial theories of the day. Newspaper reporters invariably coupled their highly colored stereotypes with frank admiration for the Indians' toughness and style. Carlisle stood for forbearance in the face of the opponents' slugging, and for open play rather than dull and deadly line blocking. (Oriard 1993, 241)

In his writing about such newspaper coverage, Oriard argues that Carlisle players were not often stereotyped as physical beings. Instead, he sees Native Americans presented as romantic icons used to make interesting copy that was perhaps insulting but not particularly harmful. Oriard provides an important contrast between the daily and weekly press coverage of Indian School athletics, but he dismisses the significance of such "implicit" racism too quickly. Though they may not have expressed biological theories of racism, is it not possible that they were just as meaningful as biological theories if we analyze them as expressions of racialized popular discourse? Could there be beneath such press coverage, just as beneath the minstrel stage that he compares it to, a desire for what Native Americans represented as a marginalized "other"?[1]

Unlike Oriard, Churchill, Hill, and Barlow argue that all popular press coverage of boarding school athletes has tended to reduce Native Americans to biological stereotypes. Churchill, Hill, and Barlow do not conduct as careful a reading of popular press articles as Oriard, but they do provide an analysis that is more sensitive to the racialized languages encoded within popular representations of non-Anglo athletes in general and Native American athletes in particular. They argue that the athletic program at Carlisle represented a commodified degradation of athletics for most Native Americans who had practiced sports within the contexts of their local social formations. At boarding school, dominant governmental and institutional bodies controlled athletics. "Thus, the individuals who participated in the Carlisle/Haskell experience may be seen to have generally relinquished direct ties with their traditional communities" (Churchill, Hill, and Barlow 1979, 27). According to Churchill and his coauthors, media images of Carlisle athletes provided a vehicle for updating older, harmful stereotypes about Native Americans:

> Insofar as the objectives of such institutions as Carlisle and Haskell were to assimilate Native American youth into the dominant culture, athletics served a distinct purpose. The Native American within non-Indian mythology is (and has always been) an overwhelmingly physical creature. Sport was and is an expedient means of processing this physicality into a "socially

acceptable" package without disrupting mythology; Indians tracked as
"Indians" into the mainstream. There could be but one result of such
manipulation: dehumanization of the Native Americans directly involved
and, by extension, dehumanization of the non-participating Native Americans whom the athletes represented in the public consciousness. Thus the
myth of the American savage was updated, all but essentially unchanged.
(Churchill, Hill, and Barlow 1979, 31)

Churchill, Hill, and Barlow recognize that stereotypes used to
describe Native American athletes, stereotypes that Oriard writes of
as relatively benign, can cause harm by preparing a general population
to accept their subjugation in the future. At the same time, however,
Churchill et al. provide a somewhat incomplete analysis, drawing, for
example, a stark line between "traditional" sports and boarding school
athletics. Boarding school sports, they write, served only one purpose and
created a single outcome. Yet if this were true, how would Churchill et al.
account for the different forms of representation that Oriard discovered
between the daily and the weekly press, or the complex, even contradictory ideas about football expressed in the public and private writings of
Pratt? Could there not be contexts in which stereotypical images might
have provided readings that diverged from the most preferred ones?
And finally, how might we reconcile the stereotype of a purely physical
Native American athlete with the ideologies of civilization and control
that mainstream sports like football were at least publicly meant to
symbolize? In addition, neither Oriard nor Churchill, Hill, and Barlow
attempt to understand how the ideas about race communicated through
sports coverage of Carlisle might have intersected with or reflected ideas
about gender, sexuality, and desire, and neither analyzes the relationship
between race and empire.

There is no doubt that Warner provided numerous examples of the
kind of stereotyping that both Oriard and Churchill et al. show pervading
popular coverage of Native American athletics. The titles themselves
of some articles—"The Indian Massacres," "Heap Big Run-Most-Fast,"
and "Red Menaces"—hardly need explanation. Although these titles were

probably not written by Warner, they nevertheless display stereotypic-
ally broken English and images of combat that evoke an overall picture of
Native Americans as savage, violent, and simple. Yet the articles by Warner cannot be read only as expressions of monolithic stereotypes; instead,
they contain conflicting ideas about the meaning of sports at boarding
schools and the relationship of athletics and education to empire.

The articles deal with various themes pertaining to Warner's
tenure at Carlisle, such as the famous football team, Warner's relationship
to the students and the school, and his experiences as track coach for
Olympic medalists such as Louis Tewanima and Jim Thorpe. In each,
Warner wrote that through pluck and hard work, the Indians he coached
overcame tremendous odds to win or play respectably, even when greatly
outweighed by and with less experience than the opposition. In Warner's
articles, the Carlisle athletes become an American success story right
out of the pages of a Horatio Alger novel. A constant theme throughout
each is the strong discipline, character, and resolve that he associated with
Carlisle students:

> When I went to the Carlisle school in 1899 as football coach, I had all of
> the prejudices of the average white, but after fourteen years of intimate
> association, I came to hold a deep admiration for the Indian and a very high
> regard for his character and capacities.... In the thousand students at
> Carlisle were boys and girls from seventy different tribes, many having
> their first contact with civilization, yet the wildest of them showed a quick-
> ness as well as willingness to learn, and gave ample evidence of courage,
> humor, ambition, tenacity and all those other instinctive qualities that are
> blandly assumed to reside solely in the white race. Especially courage!
> (Warner 1931b, 18)

Warner's reflections are sympathetic yet paternal. Although com-
plimentary of the students he encountered, he still places himself in a
position of judgment above them. He evaluates the character of Native
Americans in a way that depends upon their ability to measure up to his
terms, namely, the ideals of the Protestant work ethic and of masculine
rugged individualism. Warner wrote, for example, in the first article of

the series, "On the athletic field, where the struggle was man to man, they felt that the Indian had his first even break, and the record proves that they took full advantage of it" (Warner 1931a, 7).[2]

At the same time that Warner praised his former players for their ability to lift themselves up by their bootstraps, he colored his articles with anecdotes that recall a different, fun-loving side to his coaching experiences. In particular, the anecdotes reveal levels of wit that Warner learned from his players. For example, in the first article of the series, Warner noted that although his players were smaller than their opponents, they hit the line with unusual fierceness and courage. Yet he follows this with a discussion of what he calls "redskin wiles":

> Trick plays, however, were what the redskins loved best. Nothing delighted them more than to outsmart the palefaces. There was never a time when they wouldn't rather have won by an eyelash with some wily stratagem than by a large score with straight football. (Warner 1931a, 7)

To illustrate his point, Warner tells the story of the famous Carlisle "hidden ball trick" in which, during a game against Harvard, his players slipped a ball under the jersey of a teammate who ran all the way for a touchdown while the opposition was thrown into confusion. Warner ends the story by distancing himself and his teams from it, saying, "[W]e never considered it a strictly legitimate play and only employed it against Harvard as a good joke on the haughty Crimson players." Although Warner attempted to reestablish that football at Carlisle was meant to teach manly combat, and not necessarily trickery and deceit, he revealed somewhat contradictory sentiments as well by referring to the Harvard team as composed of "haughty Crimson players." The antics that he allowed undercut pretensions of cultural superiority in ways that he clearly seems to have enjoyed. He repeated this theme in a more complex manner in the second article of the series:

> Mimicry was another well-developed trait [among Indians], and after every Harvard game the boys had a lot of fun parodying the Cambridge accent, even those with very little English attempting the broad A. At that, however,

Harvard was the Indian idea of perfection, and whether on the field or in the schoolroom, anything very good was always commented on as the "Harvard style." (Warner 1931b, 19)

Warner's ending of this story seems to assure readers that, in spite of their mockery, the Carlisle players ultimately respected the social elites with whom they came in contact at Harvard. In fact, Pratt argued that major college football was worthwhile in large part because the travel it provided allowed members of the team to come in contact with such highbrow fineries as expensive hotels and four-star restaurants. Understood thus, their mimicry might seem to have been an expression of praise as much as a mocking of pretension, validating the importance and centrality of a northeastern Anglo-Protestant cultural elite.

On the other hand, one might see such an explanation of the team's antics as a necessary conclusion to a story that would otherwise be very disturbing. Priscilla Wald's work on Cherokee nationhood and assimilation shows that Native American mimicry of Anglo society has a deep and complex history. She argues that rather than symbolizing assimilation, the mimicry used by Cherokee societies of the early nineteenth century were a form of resistance to absorption and relocation. Wald argues that images of imitation can be extremely disrupting to a colonial perspective, for they provide a disturbing reflection of the colonizer. "The Cherokee function as the colonized . . . returning 'the look of surveillance as the displacing gaze of the disciplined, where the observer becomes the observed and "partial" representation rearticulates the whole notion of *identity* and alienates it from essence'" (Wald 1993, 82n).[3] Wald helps us recognize that the mimicry that Carlisle students performed, not only when making fun of Harvard accents but also when playing sports, evoked from audiences ambivalence even as it displayed a satisfying image of assimilation.

Warner was one of the early prototypes of the driven coach, the likes of which would later be incarnated in the form of such coaches as Knute Rockne, Woody Hayes, Lou Holtz, Bobby Knight, or Jimmy Johnson. His players at Carlisle often did not respond well to the treatment he gave them, sometimes feeling that he used harassment and humiliation to motivate players.[4] In his *Collier's* articles, Warner recalled that his style was marked by the use of profanity and that he was forced to tone down his fury to accommodate the sentiments of his players:

> Having been coached by some rather hard-boiled gents during my years as a player, I took a fairly extensive vocabulary with me to Carlisle, and made full use of it. A week went by, and then many of the best players turned in their suits and announced that they were not coming out for practice any more.... I took some time to get at the trouble, but I finally learned that they "didn't like to be cussed at." I apologized, profoundly and sincerely, and should have thanked them, too, for the rebuke made me do some hard helpful thinking, and from that day to this I have never gone in for "rough stuff." (Warner 1931b, 19)

Most significantly, this passage is about the political relationships that it implies existed between coach and player at Carlisle. Just as mimicry forces colonizers to gaze at their own images, coaching seems to have involved important levels of negotiation that, in Warner's narrative, also presented themselves as a disturbing reflection. As one who had to manage a team at firsthand, Warner apparently could not ignore the feelings of his players, feelings that were accented by racialized power relations. He wrote, "The Indian boys gave friendship slowly, for they were a suspicious lot; but once you gained their trust, they were loyal and affectionate. I found them devoted to their race" (1931b, 19).

Even though Pratt had initially hoped to promote Indian education through sports, it was, ironically, sports that in the end provided ammunition for those who sought to close down Carlisle. In 1904 the BIA dismissed Pratt as superintendent at Carlisle after he made remarks critical of the bureau. His firing led many former supporters of the school, such as Carlos Montezuma, to begin scrutinizing the management of Carlisle. Montezuma, a pan-Indian activist, doctor, and long time ally of Pratt's, had been the team physician at Carlisle, and in the 1890s he wrote to Pratt exuberant letters praising the virtues of football. In 1907, however, he received a letter from W. G. Thompson, a former disciplinarian who first coached the Carlisle football team in 1893. Thompson alleged that corruption of Carlisle athletics began with Warner's arrival in 1899. He wrote, "In 1900, as I remember, every player was paid something at the end of the season. This, of course, was in violation of the ethics of college sport and made the players professionals" (Larner 1983, reel 2). Thompson continued on, writing that athletes were permitted to stay out late, drink, and miss classes. Warner, according to Thompson, paid players for specific achievements in games, actually keeping a "schedule of prices" for touchdowns, blocked kicks, and other plays.

Montezuma ended up writing a scathing editorial, which was printed in newspapers around the country, criticizing football at Carlisle and the professionalism and corruption that he argued it represented. Although he never mentioned Warner by name, his fire was clearly directed at the legendary coach and the tactics he was alleged to have employed. Montezuma wrote, "There is no reason why the Carlisle students should be proud of the success which in 1907 attended the football efforts of a lot of hired outsiders" (Montezuma 1907). Warner responded to the editorial in December of that year, writing to the BIA that it was "a lot of sensational charges" (Warner 1907). He defended his team as true representatives of the school, and wrote, "They are as fine a body of young men morally, of as correct habits and gentlemanly demeanor as any body of school boy, or university student, athletes in the country."

Yet it was Warner's morals, not the players', that raised the most serious questions. In 1914 a joint congressional investigating committee opened hearings on corruption at the school, alleging that Pratt's replacement, Moses Friedman, was misappropriating money and mismanaging the school. Members of Congress, particularly senators from the West tired of funding boarding schools, were looking for reasons to close Carlisle's doors, and they received help from Warner's players. Football star Gus Welch (whom Warner fondly remembered in his articles as "a highly intelligent Iroquois") led a petition drive signed by more than two hundred students that called for an investigation into the use of funds collected by the Carlisle Athletic Association, which was headed by Warner. They testified that Warner sold game tickets in hotels where the team stayed, and they suggested that he kept the money; they told of the coach's common use of profanity; and they told detailed stories of Warner's gambling on the team's performance. They told of players getting special privileges while the rest of the student body suffered from inadequate food and housing and said that drinking was common among players. Jack Newcombe writes that "Warner, in Welch's judgement, was a fine coach but a man with little principle" (Newcombe 1975, 242).

Friedman and Warner were fired in 1914, and the school quickly moved away from the promotion of high-profile athletics. In June 1914 a mere three months after the congressional hearings into corruption at the school, Carlisle's monthly journal, *The Red Man*, printed an article titled "The Temptations of an Athlete," anonymously authored by "One of Them." In the article, the author argued that "although athletics can be of great benefit to a man, they can also be immensely detrimental." He (the author identified himself as a man) testified that during his collegiate athletic career, he became obsessed by sports and neglected his studies, and that sports had provided him with a false sense of superiority over other students, ruining personal and family relationships and forcing him to associate with unsavory characters:

> Often an athlete must associate with or compete against men who are foul-mouthed and evil-minded. Sometimes a bad example or a few evil words by a man whose physical powers he admires are enough to knock a young fellow off his balance and start him on the wrong track. Again, one is sometimes harmed by the low moral standards which control the team. When a coach or captain's principles allow dirty play, unfairness or crookedness, their pupils are of necessity in danger of becoming tainted. (One of Them 1914, 439)

Among the other "temptations" that greet the athlete, according to the author, are drinking, professionalism, and general dishonesty. It is probably not much of a coincidence that there is such similarity between this author's experiences and the career of "Pop" Warner. The article represents a retreat from high-profile athletics at Carlisle. Formerly a public symbol of manliness, virtue, and nobility, football had become symbolic of decadence, corruption, and dishonesty.

Warner's public memoir of his coaching career at Carlisle is a remarkable document when one considers the amount of shame that he helped to bring to the program. It represents a kind of public amnesia, or at the very least a heroic work of rehabilitation. Yet the actual corruption that drove Warner from the school is perhaps less important than its consequences. Sports historian Joseph Oxendine notes that the dramatic reaction of the federal government to the abuses documented at Carlisle contrasts greatly with the relatively permissive attitude toward "non-Indian institutions, which have encountered serious academic irregularities, professionalism, and drug abuse problems over the years" (Oxendine 1988, 202). To some degree, Oxendine has it backward. Carlisle was not closed because of irregularities in athletics. Tales of corruption within the athletic program were used by those already committed to closing the school. However, his observation is an important one, for it correctly signals how corruption within Carlisle's sports programs undermined assumptions of the moral authority of unified nationhood guided by Anglo-Protestant leadership.

Carlisle's sports history provides an important context for understanding Native American experiences in boarding schools and the role of athletics within them. At Carlisle, sports first became a significant source of good public relations, but the publicity that they generated can be read neither as a seamless tale of domination and manipulation nor as a pure expression of Indian identity. Rather, it illustrates how images of Native American athletic prowess could evoke ambivalent sentiments among a variety of audiences and interests in dominant society. Such ambivalence might allow cultural critics to understand sports as an important location at boarding schools where Native American identities and experiences gained a voice and where new identities were explored and imagined.

CHAPTER 2

# The Struggle over
# the Meaning of Sports

In January 1900 the Phoenix Indian School's newspaper, the *Native American*, reported that the Carlisle football team had stopped at the school on New Year's Eve by special invitation on their return east from a game against the University of California. Phoenix and Carlisle played a game on New Year's Day. The *Native American*, which regularly published scores and stories about Carlisle football games, on January 13, 1900, characterized it as a lopsided victory for Carlisle: "Of course our team was out of sight with the Carlisle giants, but their coach did see five among our players whom he would like to add to his number."

Just a few years after it began to receive national recognition, the athletic program at the Carlisle Indian School started to influence the superintendents of some of the other federal off-reservation boarding schools located throughout the western two-thirds of the United States. According to Joseph Oxendine, for example, Haskell Institute in Lawrence, Kansas, developed its high-profile athletic program largely because the BIA general superintendent of Indian education, H. B. Peairs, "was cognizant of the recognition that athletics had brought to Carlisle and was hopeful that the same thing could occur at Haskell" (Oxendine 1988, 195). By the 1920s Haskell's successful football and track teams led many to call it the "New Carlisle of the West" (197).

Haskell would develop one of the most famous athletic programs in the off-reservation boarding school system, but between 1900 and

31

1930 many other boarding schools made sports a core part of their curricular and extracurricular life for students. Even if they did not produce nationally recognized football teams, schools often seemed to measure their athletic programs against Carlisle's. At the very least, Carlisle showed that sports could fulfill recreational needs at a school and that they could provide a validating image of Native American education for the general public.

However, it is also important to place Carlisle's influence in a larger context, one that takes into account the rise of physical recreation as a component of American education, the commercial media's attention to sports, and the athletic heritage that Native Americans brought to schools. Although important, Carlisle did not necessarily determine the sports that were played or what they meant to students, to school officials, or to communities around boarding schools. As important as they were to promoting boarding schools and assimilation, sports spoke to students' need to play, and they addressed in complex ways the ideological goals of boarding schools as institutions.

Chapter 1 noted the ambivalence toward sports expressed by some of those who created the boarding school system. This ambivalence suggests that such powerful groups did not necessarily determine any sort of seamless meaning for boarding school athletics, even though they did attempt to use sports to advance their own careers and ideological interests.

In fact, students themselves came to boarding schools from cultures with athletic histories of their own, and according to accounts such as those by Pratt and Warner, many seem to have taken to their new sports with enthusiasm. In fact, part of the success that Warner enjoyed at Carlisle he credited to his ability to draw from the athletic cultural heritage of students who came to the school.[1]

Sports became a prominent part of boarding school life during the first decades of the twentieth century in large part because during this historical period, recreation came to be seen as a necessary part of any formal education, and athletics emerged as a dominant form of popular culture in the United States at large. In annual reports in the decades immediately before and after the turn of the century, boarding school superintendents repeatedly expressed their wishes for recreational equipment and playground space as an urgent need, not as a luxury. They connected both sports and recreation with concerns for the physical and mental health of students, a great many of whom were, in fact, suffering from such diseases as tuberculosis and trachoma while at school (Child 1993, 156–92). In his annual report for 1890 to the commissioner of Indian affairs, for example, Charles Francis Meserve, superintendent of Haskell, wrote,

> There is no gymnasium or place where instruction can be given in physical training. An educational institution at the present day is scarcely deserving of the name, unless it is furnished with a gymnasium fitted up with all the modern conveniences for carrying on successfully the best physical training. (*Annual Report of the Commissioner of Indian Affairs*, 1890, 292)

School administrators seem to have identified outdoor recreation as a particularly important method for addressing health problems at schools. In 1912 the Phoenix *Native American* printed a number of articles about tuberculosis, indicating that it had become a serious problem at the school. In the September 14 issue, for example, the paper announced that October 27 had been declared by the National Association for the Study and Prevention of Tuberculosis as "Tuberculosis Day." Earlier that year, on June 29, the paper had printed an article stating that mild exercise was an appropriate part of the cure for tuberculosis among Native Americans, even though the standard treatment for Anglos called exclusively for rest. The paper explained the difference in approaches, writing,

> [An Indian boy or girl] will fret and fume more [than white children], and so stir up the system more, than if a moderate amount of exercise is allowed. So the "rules of the books" in regard to rest in tuberculosis, are not closely followed in the treatment of these Indians. Such rules are often made by men who have thought too long, too minutely and perhaps too scientifically on the physical aspects of tuberculosis and in doing so have banished human considerations too completely from the case.... All the boys and

girls of school age, who are in the incipient stage of tuberculosis, attend the half-day outdoor school; this keeps them pleasantly and usefully occupied. They take moderate exercise—the girls help the matron in sewing and mending, the boys do light work on the grounds. Games not requiring much strength are played and general recreation is encouraged.

This quotation came at a time when the BIA had ordered boarding schools to actively address the problem of tuberculosis. Although the recommendation in this passage runs against standard procedure, it is important to recognize that there was really no reliable way of treating the disease during this period. It had only been since 1865 that doctors had established tuberculosis as a contagious disease, and Robert Koch had only located its bacteria in 1882. It would not be until the 1950s that any effective medical cure would be developed. In 1912 most doctors accepted that the most effective way of controlling tuberculosis was prevention by isolating infected patients. The very nature of boarding schools, however, tended to mix infected with noninfected children in overcrowded, often unsanitary conditions. This created situations where the disease was allowed to spread. In addition, because students were living in unfamiliar environments and under strict forms of discipline, they were often under great mental and physical stress, which could make latent cases active. Diane Putney has argued in her examination of tuberculosis and federal health policy for Native Americans that treatment programs for the disease more often reflected ideological perspectives and political climates than any real cure (Putney 1980).

The passage suggesting that recreation be part of a tuberculosis-treatment regimen illustrates the fact that outdoor exercise had become associated with health during this era. Such ideas were not unique to educators at boarding schools for Native Americans. In fact, they had become particularly popular among urban social workers and reform-minded activists working in overcrowded cities. The movement to build playgrounds in cities, endorsed by settlement-house workers such as Jane Addams, as well as by President Theodore Roosevelt, helped to make playgrounds one of the most significant aspects of urban design between

1900 and the end of World War I (Gorn and Goldstein 1993, 176–77). Such social reformers shared with boarding school promoters a concern with the assimilation of impoverished, non-English-speaking, or non-white populations.

Superintendent Peairs reflected this belief in the importance of outdoor play at an address to a conference of boarding school supervisors held in Lawrence, Kansas, in 1912. In a portion of his speech reprinted in the *Native American* of October 12, he stated, "More emphasis has been placed on the physical development and health of Indian pupils during the past year than at any other time during the history of Indian education. Outdoor play ground apparatus has been furnished for many of the boarding schools and for even a large number of day schools." The conference concluded with a number of resolutions, among them that "[a] deeper personal interest should be taken in the social and ethical welfare of Indian pupils.... Work of this nature should be under the supervision of competent persons who will, with the assistance of all other employees, lend their presence and set a proper example in manners and dress." In addition to resolving that schools would provide more "practical lessons in thrift and economy," would more closely supervise students' spending of money, and would teach "self-reliance and individual responsibility," the conference concluded "that suitable equipment for outdoor playgrounds [should] be installed at all boarding and day schools, to be used under intelligent supervision, and that the holding of academic classes out of doors [should] be encouraged."

In his speech, Peairs reflected ideas about sports consistent with those of reformers during the Progressive Era. He suggested that physical recreation would improve not only physical health but also moral character, and that it would promote the ideals of delayed gratification, hard work, and individual responsibility.

In practice, playground recreation tended to be provided more for girls than for boys, whereas the values of individuality that Peairs associated with physical exercise were more directed toward male students. Boarding school curricula of the first decades of the twentieth century held fast to Victorian notions of proper gender behavior. This meant that girls were taught to be the caretakers of the family, nurturing their husbands' and children's moral purity and Godly virtue. The superintendent of the Phoenix Indian School, S. M. McCowan, summarized this belief in a "Talk to the Girls," which was published in the first edition of the *Native American*, on January 13, 1900:

> I have the old fashioned reverence for the girl. To me she stands for the sweeter, gentler side of life. The boy is the rough, restless element, full of tireless energy, seeking opportunities for a display of bold, spirited deeds. The girl represents home, quiet, rest, and content. She it is who touches our moral nature and makes us gentler, kinder, more manly.... The most charming girl in all the world is the broad, generous, sympathetic one— the purely unselfish one—the girl who thinks more of others than herself, who is always considerate of the feelings of others.

The sort of unselfishness being promoted among girls is a far cry from the competitive individualism male students often report having felt at boarding schools, and it certainly contrasts with a later Phoenix superintendent's complaint that one of the core faults of Native Americans is their "willingness to share" (Skinner 1958). Photographs of children playing in boarding school playgrounds often show girls playing and sometimes identify a playground as being specifically for girls. Indeed, the girls do not appear to be participating in any kind of competitive sport that, like football, promotes individualistic tenacity and grit. Instead, they play on swings, Maypoles, and jungle gyms in what appear to be cooperative and peaceful ways. Even competitive teams that were designed for girls, like the Pipestone (Minnesota) Indian School's basketball teams, would have played under rules designed specifically for the women's game to promote "feminine" traits like nurturing, teamwork, and selflessness (Cahn 1993).

Outdoor play and recreation at boarding school, therefore, did not always connote competitive individualism. Ideas of appropriate feminine and masculine behavior promoted in the boarding school curricula, along with behavioral expectations associated more generally with sports, some-times conflicted with this goal, promoting selfless femininity over indi-viduality. As illustrated in Chapter 1, the strict discipline and control of sexuality exercised at boarding schools can be read as also revealing fears on the part of the dominant society of repressed desires and passions, fears that were commonly projected upon colonized populations. That such policies represented deep tensions within the dominant society also suggests that those dominated might have been able to find spaces for agency within the uncertainties and fault lines that existed within domi-nant ideologies.

The early twentieth century was the time when sports around the industrialized world began to emerge as a primary site for the creation of spectacle. In the United States, it was the time when grand football sta-diums and baseball palaces were built, when mass media discovered the gripping power of athletics for mass audiences, and when audiences forged new identities and expressed new passions through the admira-tion of athletic heroes and teams. For boarding school students, and for Native Americans more generally, sporting events also created a context for the celebration of intertribal cooperation and identity, sometimes on a scale rarely ever seen before. It was the possibility of such spectacle that served as the backdrop of one of the largest intertribal celebrations in twentieth-century Native American history, the 1926 homecoming at Haskell Institute.

## The Haskell Homecoming of 1926

Between 1925 and 1926, motivated in large part by the success and national fame of the Haskell football team during the 1920s, Native Americans from across the United States launched a massive fund-raising campaign to construct a new, 10,500-seat stadium on Haskell's campus. They ultimately raised between $180,000 and $250,000, and in the fall of 1926 the new venue was ready. That Halloween weekend, representatives of more than seventy tribes and nations gathered at Haskell to dedicate the stadium in what promised to be the most spectacular homecoming celebration any Indian boarding school had ever seen. In addition to the game scheduled on Saturday between Haskell and Bucknell College, the festivities were to take place over three days and include a powwow, traditional Native American dances, and gatherings of tribes in their traditional clothing.

The 1926 homecoming and stadium dedication has become one of the most important events in twentieth-century Indian boarding school history. The stadium still stands on the Haskell campus (now known as the Haskell Indian Nations University), and images of the celebration have been publicly displayed in exhibits and books. There are a number of different ways that scholars have interpreted the meaning of this event (or of similar events that celebrate ethnic or cultural identity). Historian Oxendine has written about the Haskell homecoming as a modern continuation of ancient Native American traditions that brought together large groups for feasts and celebrations surrounding an athletic event such as a footrace or a ball game:

> As in earlier centuries, an athletic contest ... brought together the Indian community as perhaps nothing else could have done. The importance and appropriateness of athletics as a major social event for Indians was still apparent well into the twentieth century. However, it was no longer the Blackfeet against the Cheyenne or the Cherokee against the Sauk and the Fox, all Indians joined together against a common foe (i.e., non-Indians). The elders, too, recognized that they were no longer each other's enemies. It was clear that a new day had arrived. (Oxendine 1988, 201)

For Oxendine, the Haskell homecoming represents a kind of public ritual in which Indian nations acknowledged their intertribal connections, connections that would increasingly come to define Native American social and political life in the twentieth century. He sees this not as a mark of any sort of loss of identity but, rather, as the continuation of long-standing tradition, simply in a new form. Although not many others have written about this particular event, some scholars have developed theories about similar forms of ethnic expression.

To another group of thinkers, celebrations such as the Haskell homecoming are more of a last hurrah than continuations of past tradition. According to this point of view, characterized for example in the work of social historian John Higham, this event should be seen as a ritual of integration into society in which markers of tradition and history are part of an overall struggle to fit group identity into the larger national unity (Higham 1984). One could go even further and argue that the pow-wow was allowed as part of the homecoming because Native American identities and cultural practices were no longer a threat, or did not pose any sort of oppositional meaning, within dominant society. Instead, when coupled with a homecoming football game, they became a sign of acceptance into a pluralistic yet coherent national unity.

There are some problems with understanding the homecoming celebration in this manner, with concluding only that the intertribal celebration was little more than an expression of nostalgia. Such interpretations certainly create neat, progressive, linear narratives of assimilation and integration into dominant society, but they do not adequately account for the diverse ways in which events such as the powwow have actually been experienced and interpreted. As April Schultz has argued in her work on ethnic identity among Norwegian Americans in the early part of the twentieth century, such interpretations attempt to "explain away" contradictions that get in the way of a story with a clear sense of closure. Employing an interpretation that sees ethnic celebrations as engaged in cultural dialogues involving contestation and debate, Schultz argues that ethnic identity is not something to be preserved or lost. Rather, such celebrations reflect processes of negotiation among factions within a community, as well as those within dominant society. They embody "contradictory visions of the past and, therefore, of [the] present and [the] future" (Schultz 1994, 9–13).

There is not much available that would give historians and cultural scholars direct insight into the visions that Native Americans had of the homecoming celebration. However, Anglo political leaders, educators, and clergy left behind much that certainly reveals contradictions surrounding the ways that the celebration represented the past, the present, and the future. At issue was the plan to allow an intertribal powwow to be a part of the celebration. For some, this was a positive step, a sign that Native Americans had come to accept their place as citizens. For others, however, the powwow represented a retreat, a concession to what some termed reactionary forces within Native American communities who did not accept the "progress" that boarding schools were supposed to foster and who could be easily exploited as local color for non-Indian spectators.

One of those who objected to the Haskell celebration was E. D. Mossman, superintendent from the Standing Rock Agency in Fort Yates, North Dakota. After receiving a circular pamphlet announcing the event, Mossman wrote to the commissioner of Indian affairs, Charles H. Burke, to express his protest. Among other things, Mossman objected to four pictures on the cover of a circular, pictures that he said "depict[ed] the Indian as he was and as many of them would still love to be." (He did not describe the circular beyond this.) Mossman went on to argue that it should have pictured more desirable role models, such as those of the "farmer, laborer or business man." Echoing Pratt's rhetoric, he wrote of the average Native American,

> Either he [sic] must be taken into the body politic as a citizen like other citizens or he must perish.... The Indian loves to look backward and in my opinion this celebration is a most decisive backward step. On this reservation as on many others the bane of our educational, health and industrial program is this same inclination to Pow Pow. (Mossman 1926)

Mossman went on to write that the inclusion of an "Indian village" where Native peoples would eat "squaw bread" and "squat around the fire," as well as the display of traditional Indian dances, would only serve to enhance the position of "reactionary" elements among tribes who resisted the "progressive" guidance of "Christian Indians, missionaries or educators."

The Reverend Henry H. Treat from the Red Stone Mission in Anadarko, Oklahoma, expressed a similar dismay over the homecoming celebrations. Treat was particularly upset by the dances to be performed at the celebration. Expressing both a race and a class bias, he wrote to Burke,

> I am hurt, as were all of us missionaries, that just because of a desire for a great crowd at this home coming to Haskell, it should seem to be necessary to undo the work of thirty five years of attempt to help make these Kiowa, Comanche, and others, Christian citizens. We believe that the Department and the School have put themselves on a level with the cheap John white trash of these parts who make rodeos and picnics and keep the Indians going from one dance to another all the summer long. (Treat 1926)

Treat sent Burke a copy of a resolution drafted by the Annual Conference of Indian Missionary Workers that met in Anadarko on October 19 and 20, 1926. In it, the missionaries characterized traditional Native American dances as "subversive of the teachings of the Christian religion, and of the best that is being developed in the lives of the Indian people." The conference resolved that such "Indian customs and practices which we are constantly opposing among our people ... are highly detrimental to their economic, moral and religious advancement" (Resolution from the Annual Conference of Missionary Workers 1926).

H. B. Peairs defended his decision to allow such a celebration of Native American cultures by explaining how it fit into the progressive narratives that guided federal Indian policy:

> There is no more effective method of teaching a lesson on any subject than by means of making comparisons and contrasts. The program rendered at Haskell certainly was an opportunity to put on several contests which did very positively show progress of Indians through education. (Peairs 1926)

In other words, the display of war dances and "costume" by visiting tribes could be framed as a kind of picturesque relic of the past. Publicly presented, it could demonstrate the evolutionary ideology that guided federal Indian educational policy. The entire celebration could provide a stage for showing Haskell students as formerly primitive beings, earnestly and successfully struggling to gain a foothold on civilization. Far from preserving traditions, the presentation of Native American culture in the present, as a kind of entertainment for white football audiences, could actually cement Native Americans in the past by rendering those traditions meaningless—little more than decorative display. Peairs hoped popular representations would present Indian cultures as a thing of the past.

This kind of presentation, or framing, was particularly important at the historical moment of the homecoming. In 1924, only two years before the dedication of the stadium, Native Americans had been granted federal citizenship. This development, however, was not something that all Native peoples accepted as something positive. Although it did grant many tribal members new rights, it also burdened them with many more responsibilities (like military service and taxation), and for some it created legal loopholes that made it easier for the federal government or private interests to buy or confiscate tribal lands. Recognizing this, some tribes refused to accept citizen status.

On one hand, Indian boarding school administrators like Peairs wanted to demonstrate that the next generation of Native Americans was "ready" for and willingly accepted the implications of citizenship. This meant not only that they would be able to wear starched clothing and speak English but also that they would accept the status they were being trained for at schools like Haskell. As Lomawaima (1993 and 1994) has illustrated, students at boarding schools, particularly after the turn of the century, were not trained to compete for success as future professionals, business leaders, or scholars. Rather, they were trained in both the practical skills and work discipline of blue-collar labor. The curriculum at most boarding schools focused mostly upon learning a vocational trade. For girls, this meant a form of domestic or secretarial labor, such as cooking, sewing, ironing, or typing. Boys learned mechanical skills, carpentry, and farming techniques. For both, boarding school equated citizen status for Native Americans with entering society at the bottom rung.

The intertribal powwow, however, did not communicate to all

audiences what Peairs might have hoped and imagined. Two print media sources, the local press and the Indian service (which printed the Haskell weekly newspaper and the stadium program on the day of the game), illustrated the extent to which administrators like Peairs were successful, and the extent to which they were not successful, in "framing" this event. Papers like the *Kansas City Times, Kansas City Star, Kansas City Journal, Topeka Daily State Journal,* and *Muskogee Daily Phoenix* all provided extensive coverage of the weekend festivities, including feature stories and captioned front-page photographs. In some of their accounts of the pow-wow and homecoming, Indian service publications and newspapers associated the event with humor, nostalgia, historical narratives of social advancement, and examples of "good sportsmanship" that affirmed ideas linking Indian education to progress. Other times, however, the local press provided sensational accounts of the event that portrayed displays and expressions as shocking and sexually provocative. What seemed to interest these members of the press corps were not the displays of disciplined progress but those displays that seemed to resist the very values and behavioral norms with which progress had become associated.

On October 29, the day before the main event, the *Kansas City Journal* published a spread that was somewhat typical of what the other newspapers in the area printed. It included a series of five photographs on page 3 of their front section the Friday before the game under the headline "Lawrence Harks Back to Frontier Days as Indians 'Take' City for the Biggest Pow Wow in History." The photos progress from left to right (numbered 1 through 5) and are framed below by the following caption:

> Indians have captured Lawrence again. But this time it is a pleased Lawrence that watches the influx of representatives of fifty tribes attending the biggest Pow Wow in history on the campus of the Haskell Indian Institute. Above are typical scenes of the Pow Wow.

The first photo shows a portrait of the Osage chief Bacon Rind. It is followed by a photo of Blackfeet Indians in traditional clothing doing a war dance. The third photo represents a kind of transition, an ironic juxtaposition of an Indian chief dressed in fringed leather leaning against the hood of a car. The caption highlights the irony of this image: "A chief bows to Father Time and substitutes a modern war horse for his traditional pony." This image and caption do not just convey humor; they do so by presenting modern technology as a natural component of the progress of time. This further positions Native American traditions as a relic of the past that, in a practical sense, are incompatible with the present. The fourth photo is of the baby who won the "baby contest," dressed in a white lace outfit, and the final photo is of "Miss Hazel Dupuis," the beauty queen winner, who wears makeup and is dressed in a fur-lined coat, fashionable hat, and dress.

This progressive vision was an implicit part of representations that characterized other, less explicitly narrative press descriptions of this event. They emerged particularly in descriptions of the Blackfeet war dances that took place that weekend. The October 29, 1926, *Muskogee Daily Phoenix*, for example, printed its own photo of the dance. The caption read:

> Hoop-la, the Redskins are out for scalps again! But only in athletic contests this time. With thousands of Indians celebrating—one of the chief events being a war dance contest—a $250,000 stadium at Haskell Institute, Lawrence, Kansas, now is duly dedicated and ready for "warfare."

The Muskogee representation of the war dance is very similar to that provided in the *Kansas City Journal*: Both make light of it as no longer threatening. Football is established as the modern replacement for war. Unlike war, however, the outcome of a football game has no really lasting consequences—no land is ceded, nobody (hopefully) is killed, no treaties need to be signed. These war dances, then, could be observed safely and even humorously by the largely white readership of the newspaper. That they were safe to observe conveyed the impression that an era of Indian resistance was over; indeed, that its passing could be nostalgically lamented.

The Indian service press newspaper at Haskell, The *Indian Leader*, which published both the official game program and an extensive postgame issue, also depicted the event in this manner. The cover of the program is an artistic rendering of an Indian chief in floor-length feather headdress and fringed leather shirt and leggings. He passes the newly built Haskell football stadium in his arms to a young Indian boy, himself wearing only a loincloth, moccasins, and two feathers in his braided hair. They stand on a bluff overlooking a grassy pasture. The passage printed inside the program itself contains a theme repeated in press clippings of the day, expressing amazement that such a friendly gathering of Indians and whites could take place only fifty years after the Battle of Little Big Horn (which had been in the summer of 1876):

> Haskell Institute is the largest Indian school in the world. Its mission is the fitting of young Indian men and women for the problems of life which white civilization has brought to the Indian race. When one stops to consider that Haskell Institute is dedicating a huge stadium just fifty years after ancestors of its pupils fought at the battle of Little Big Horn, some idea of the huge success of Indian education can be gathered. (*Indian Leader: Haskell Celebration Official Program* 1926, 21)

After the game, the next issue of the *Indian Leader*, of October 29–November 19, declared that the pregame festivities and the game itself "presented a thrilling pictorial scene, mingling the past, the present, and the future." As did the popular press, the *Indian Leader* took special note of the Blackfeet dances:

> A band of Blackfeet in ceremonial costume, arriving Wednesday, October 27, lent picturesqueness to the Pow-Wow and reminded crowds of the rapid rise of the Indian race in the last few decades from the days of prairie warfare to the dedication of a school stadium, comparable to many of the magnificent college stadiums of the country.

Together, these visual and verbal images not only represent Native

American culture nostalgically, but they also portray Indian resistance as no longer existent. They implicitly or explicitly construct a historical narrative. Such public chronicles of the homecoming festivities interpreted the powwow itself as an implicit endorsement of boarding school education. The display of traditional dancing and clothing, in such texts, confirms a narrative of progress in which elders representing their vanishing race come to observe their modern children.

Such progressive narratives were also a part of the coverage of the actual game between Haskell and Bucknell played during the homecoming weekend. Accounts of Indian sportsmanship were a part of both Indian service and popular press coverage of the game. The game program, for example, describes Haskell's head football coach, R. E. Hanley, as someone whose leadership "won [Haskell] the reputation of being hard, clean fighters who often fight their way up from behind to win." The *Indian Leader*'s postgame issue reprinted the following letter from the *Topeka Daily State Journal* of November 1, 1926, also praising Haskell for good sportsmanship. It focuses on behavior of fans, but importantly, it links this in the end to gentlemanly virtue:

> The Haskell Institute last Saturday set a precedent for a football contest that might well be followed by other institutions of learning throughout the country. On arriving at the Haskell grounds and in the Indian village one noticed scores of football fans wearing little tags upon which were the words, "welcome Bucknell." ... This courtesy to a visiting football team appeared to be a marked contrast to such phrases as "Twist the Tiger's Tail," "Beat the Jayhawks," "Beat the Teachers," and countless other expressions. Football, like other sports, can be played hard and for all that is in it, but courtesy is the first step for a gentleman and an institution to take.

If such an article conveys an unwritten story of progress and success, it also contains an important irony. By comparing the good sportsmanship of Haskell fans to the behavior of University of Missouri or University of Kansas fans (as implied in references to "the Tiger" and "Jayhawks"), it asserts that the Indian students have held themselves to and achieved a higher standard of decorum than non-Indian students. One could interpret this as portraying a particularly comforting image of the Native American male as a racial type. The control that Indian men maintained over their passions within a violent and often provocative game like football confirmed for many that an era of real battle had passed and that, provided Indians had the proper, white, paternal leader like Hanley, Indians and whites could knock heads on the football field and walk away with no hard feelings—mutually respecting the boundaries between legitimate competition and illegitimate violence. Yet it might also be seen as revealing the kind of ambivalence (noted in chapter 1) in which the passions contained within good sportsmanship represented precisely what many Anglo audiences most desired, and at the same time feared, within themselves.

Such popular representations of the Haskell homecoming suggest Peairs succeeded in his effort to frame the powwow and dances within an overall narrative of progress, but there is also evidence that the sort of ambivalence buried beneath representations of sportsmanship disrupted this narrative. Many articles about the weekend's festivities did not construct a neat, progressive narrative but instead were sensational accounts that actually confirmed some of the worst fears held by the pastors and ministers who protested against the powwow. These newspaper stories portrayed the visitors to Lawrence that weekend as wild, even out of control. They circulated images of the pregame festivities as exotic, strange, and sexually exhilarating. An article in the October 30, 1926, *Kansas City Times* best exemplifies this portrayal of the event. Under the headline "Like Birds and Beasts," the article describes the Friday-night dances at the stadium:

> It seemed tonight as if the slinking animals of field and forest and the birds of mountain crag and wood, possessed of demons, came out into the area of the Haskell stadium to dance to frog noises from the Wkarusa and the sobbing cadence of wind.... Aye-yah-aye-yah sing the ... Osages, Pawnees.... Only the must colored blankets around rounded backs are seen, but the measure excites the heart.... Feathers become tumultuous.

Knees bend grotesquely; moccasined feet descend toe downward; arms rise and fall. Beribboned weapons are twirled and swung menacingly. But the dance is stopped before ecstacy comes. Enough is enough.

This journalist paints a scene of uncontained emotions. His description of the dances is almost explicitly sexual. The passage makes the event seem as if the spectators were on the verge of experiencing a mass orgasm. Unlike the accounts of gentlemanly behavior on the football field and in the stands, this article portrays the event as an almost totally unrepressed outpouring of shockingly passionate expression:

The animals and birds, squaws and children, sweep over the shadowy field in an inter-tribal dance, the combined tom-toms thundering, the grandstands echoing. It is Custer's last stand, the Halloween of beasts and birds. There is madness in the air. It would not be weird in the sunlight, but in a strip of dim light on a dark night and the air clouded with fogs of a thousand cigarettes, it was diabolism.

These descriptions not only make the dances seem dangerous; they portray them as exotic and sexually attractive. This author portrays the powwow, under the smoke-filtered light of a football stadium at night, as being an experience that was simultaneously terrifying and intensely pleasurable. I would argue that this is far more a reflection of cultural tensions within the dominant society than of anything inherently sexual or exotic in the dances themselves. Rawick and Roediger show that Europeans projected their repressed desires onto those whom they encountered from Africa; this account reveals a similar transference of desires that many who attended the powwow perhaps felt were unmet in their lives but also could not allow themselves to express or freely acknowledge.

In this manner the powwow was indeed threatening, not because it might provoke any sort of violent insurrection, but because it evoked repressed desires. The Indian dances of that evening were followed by a display of physical education, hygiene, and gymnastics by female students who attended Haskell. This was to provide a comparison between the untamed past and the modern present. Yet the newspaper article's account of the evening represents the display as somewhat anticlimactic compared to the dances that had taken place earlier:

> Seventy-five Haskell girls in black bloomers and white blouses did the dance of health—gymnastics—for the benefit of the big chiefs. They marched, formed a giant letter H; did sitting up exercises.

Lomawaima has illustrated the significance of bloomers, like those described in the last portion of the dance, to boarding school education. She argues that they were associated with control of female sexuality and the body, and that such control was tied to a more general lesson of subservience under regimented authority (Lomawaima 1994, 98–99). However, compared to the lurid descriptions of the "Halloween of beasts and birds," the formation of a giant letter H is almost comically boring. This journalist presents progress as dead and the supposedly bygone rituals of Native American life as exciting and alive. No doubt this was not the journalist's intention. But no matter how unwittingly, the descriptions of sexually uncontrolled savages also reveal the intense repression that "civilization" implied.

Unlike the picturesque noble savage presented by the Indian service and in other popular accounts, these Indians still needed to be tamed. Their identities as Indians were presented not as a thing of the past but as something that was "menacingly" alive in the present. This is the irony of the progressive representations that guided the coverage of Indian boarding school sports. The motifs employed often made the "past" more alive than the progressive narrative itself. In addition, it identified Indians not as assimilated beings but as Indians battling and often winning against white foes on a symbolic field of battle.

These media representations only let us see what whites thought of these events. But the conflicts they evoke provide clues to the ways Indians might have found sports at boarding schools important. Only twelve years after this event, Haskell discontinued its major college football schedule. With the administration of John Collier at the BIA during the 1930s, Indian schools placed less emphasis on public, high-profile, interscholastic competition and more emphasis on intramural athletics and physical education. Such moves were made with the well-intentioned motive of ending the exploitation of Indian athletes by overzealous coaches and school administrators. However, a consequence of such moves may have also been the severance of an important cultural resource for Native Americans within the context of their lives during the twentieth century. As Lomawaima writes of Chilocco Indian School, although it was created by and for white people, "[i]t was, however, an institution inhabited by Indian students, who created its everyday life. Every student knew Chilocco was an Indian school" (1994, 98–99). On the Saturday of the dedication, Haskell trounced Bucknell 36–0. But the spectacle that football allowed before the game also made it clear that Haskell was an Indian school, and its football victories were ones by and for Native Americans throughout the United States.

CHAPTER 3

# The 1930s and Pan-Indian Pride

> I think that's the only thing we felt that we were equal on.
> That the only thing that they see us as being equal were—we
> played them and we beat them. You get the impression . . . they
> already got us beat just by looking at us. But then we end up
> beating them and they see how good we are, it . . . makes them
> think of more respect for us, you know?
>
> —*Jeff McCloud, interview, May 10, 1995*

Jeff McCloud, a social worker in Minneapolis, attended a boarding school during the late 1960s, fifty years after Carlisle closed and forty years after the Haskell homecoming, yet his insights into the importance of the pride gained from athletic teams have applied to many subjugated groups for much of the past 120 years. Just as the loyalties that sports create might work in the service of prevailing national narratives, they can also be a powerful expression of alternative narratives and identities for groups who do not find their points of view reflected in dominant representations. In combat and victory, Native Americans, African Americans, Chicanas and Chicanos, and others have gained immense pride in their shared identities rooted in historical experiences of marginalization, discrimination, and disenfranchisement. This pride is important, for it can allow such groups to combat the invisibility that they often face in mainstream society by imagining a common source of inspiration.[1]

I met Jeff McCloud in the spring of 1995 when I was conducting research for this book. He contacted me by phone, calling long distance to respond to an advertisement that I had taken out in a Native American newspaper asking for volunteers to participate in an oral history project on sports and federal Indian boarding schools. McCloud had left a message on my home answering machine in which he told me that he had

51

been a good athlete but had never played on any boarding school teams because he had refused to cut his hair. Upon hearing the message, I picked up the phone and tried frantically, but in vain to reach him at the number he had left. He had already told me enough to let me guess that he might have some valuable insights.

Fortunately, I was finally able to reach McCloud, and I arranged an interview with him at his office in the Minneapolis Division of Indian Work, where he was employed as a director of social services to the city's large Native American population. He had some paradoxical reflections upon his experiences in boarding school, ones that tell us a great deal about the complexities of sports and these institutions. McCloud came to Flandreau Indian School from an Omaha reservation near the city of Omaha, Nebraska. When he was old enough to go to high school, he had the choice of going to a predominantly white high school near his home, a reservation school, or to the Flandreau boarding school. He chose Flandreau, and he believes that he "probably wouldn't have graduated from high school" if he had not done so. However, he is also critical of his experiences there. He said that the school curriculum itself was not intellectually challenging, nor was it respectful of students' desires to attend college or do any work other than manual labor.

Like many other Native Americans who grew up during the late 1950s and 1960s, he lived in a relatively urban environment, and his cultural references came not only from his reservation but also from the urban popular culture with which he grew up. He recalled that the urban Indians at Flandreau tended to hang out together, listened to Motown and African American recording artists, dressed in fashionable clothing, and had a generally more rebellious attitude than the students from more rural backgrounds. In reference to sports, the late 1960s provided students with a number of rebel-heros who were popular among students. He wove memories of Native American football stars like Roman Gabriel and Sonny Sixkiller with names like Muhammad Ali and Joe Namath. Although many of his observations reflected trends in boarding school management and policy that had been present since the system had been created, he also told of rebellious peer groups that formed at school around drinking, popular music, and dating, groups that drew from the cultural resources of the 1960s and that always contained a subversive edge.

His stories illustrate an outcome of the power structures of boarding school life, an outcome noted by Brenda Child, Tsianina Lomawaima, and Sally Hyer. That is, although the schools were designed to promote assimilation, they also created conditions that made possible new identities to be formed around rebellious subcultures, hybrid identities derived from region, tribe, or campus culture. These student peer groups allowed those attending boarding schools to forge pan-Indian alliances and identities, even though most never lost sight of the specific histories of their own nations and tribes of origin.

These outcomes were particularly dramatized in McCloud's memories of sports at Flandreau. Athletic teams were a core part of student life and culture when he was there. In an interview on May 10, 1995, he recalled that the school had good cross-country and track teams and that basketball games and wrestling matches attracted large crowds of students. He said that most students who were good athletes went out for sports and that his rebellion against getting his hair cut short was an individual decision. Yet it was one that came out of a recognition of collective circumstances that his peers faced at boarding school:

> I think it was my sophomore ... year where I connected that they were trying to makes us be, um, white. They were trying to make us live in white society. We had to dress nice, and we had to wear our clothes tucked in. We had to wear our hair short because this is how white people wanted us to look, to be like that. This is how they were, you know, short hair. If you're going to get anywhere, you need to have short hair, you know, you can't wear long hair.... I wasn't going to be that way ... conform to that. Although that's not what they said it was, but that's what, how I seen it.

McCloud recognized in sports an unstated ideological pressure to assimilate, which he felt compelled to resist. He said that most athletes at the school tended to accept lessons of conformity that he rebelled against.

He acknowledged that, for some athletes, conformity seemed to lead to a measure of upward mobility and individual success later in life. However, he also felt that for most, the lessons learned on the athletic field were empty ones. "Most of them I know of just going back to the reservation, and that's where they probably still are. A lot of them probably are dead from drinking, or from alcohol problems." McCloud observes the same "false promises" that social critics like Stanley Aronowitz have associated with working-class education and a socialization that demand self-denial in order to achieve the elusive promise of future success and happiness, and he clearly associates sports with this ethic.

Ironically, however, McCloud also recalled that sports provided him and others with a way to imagine his current circumstances critically. He cited the competitive aspect of athletic teams as crucially important to their appeal and importance at boarding school. Making a team, he said, meant "competing against other tribes ... other tribes for the same position on a team ... you beat out people from, from, um, Standing Rock or Turtle Mountain or ... trying to get the same position you're after." Yet as much as competing against other tribes was important, "to play and beat white teams was even a higher achievement." He had proud memories of the success of the school's basketball, wrestling, and cross-country teams, of competing and winning against larger high schools in Sioux Falls, and even of a "near riot" that broke out after one close game when the Native American fans felt their team had been the victim of unfair officiating.

McCloud's stories illustrate the power of the cultural and national narratives that can be carried through sports, as well as the conflicts and ironies that sports evoke between assimilation and national pride. Nationalism for subjugated groups is an important resource that provides them with a position from which they might recognize truths about their lives in the United States, truths that more conventional histories conceal. For McCloud, the pride he developed as a fan of Indian athletic teams at Flandreau helped him to critically read the pain and degradation of contemporary life on and off Indian reservations as something other than a flaw in Native American character or the inevitable outcome of historical progress. This was also true for many young Native Americans who attended boarding school decades before McCloud, and particularly during the tumultuous decade of the 1930s.

## Federal Indian Boarding Schools during the 1930s

Recent scholarship on boarding schools for Native Americans has begun to critically focus upon the 1930s as a crucial time when new possibilities emerged for the creative expression of identity by students at these institutions (see Child 1993; Hyer 1990; Lomawaima 1994). These possibilities included the boarding school sports, whose role contained contradictions and often changed between 1890 and 1950. This became particularly true after 1928, when a commission headed by Lewis Meriam issued a scathing report that criticized the wretched conditions at many schools, the highly regimented, military-style discipline they employed, and the lack of respect payed to diverse Native American cultures and traditions (Meriam et al. 1928). Among the commission's criticisms was that students lacked time for free play and recreation. With the appointment of Will Carson Ryan as director of education in 1930, and John Collier as commissioner of Indian affairs in 1933, the BIA set out to reform and ultimately to eliminate the boarding school system, heeding many of the Meriam Report's recommendations (Szasz 1977).[2]

Ryan and Collier were critical of the sports programs that had developed at boarding schools. By the early 1930s an institutional split developed over the use of sports at boarding schools. Many local school administrators and former coaches enjoyed the local notoriety and culture created by interscholastic athletics. Against their best wishes, however, national leaders such as Collier and Ryan opposed this use of sports and favored the promotion of intramural athletics and recreation, which would allow a greater degree of free play and incorporate a larger number of participants.

Meanwhile, by the 1930s the position of boarding school in the lives of Native Americans had also changed. Before this period, a great many Native Americans resisted sending their children off to boarding schools, or resisted being sent themselves. Such resistance did not end during the

1930s, but many more parents actively chose to send their children to boarding school during this decade. In part, this was because the Great Depression had a devastating impact upon Native American communities. Boarding schools offered many a form of relief, providing children with such basic necessities as food and shelter. Brenda Child notes that in addition, however, the high enrollments during this time were a response to the very effort of the federal government to shut them down, and particularly to campaigns to integrate Native American children into public schools. Child writes, "Indian students often complained that racism was the reason they chose boarding schools over public schools in Wisconsin and Minnesota. The intertribal environment attracted students who otherwise had to deal with discrimination at their local schools" (Child 1993, 64).

A graduate of the Chilocco Indian School in northern Oklahoma expressed this sentiment during an oral history interview with me on April 21, 1995. He had attended Chilocco during the 1930s and recalled that the all-Indian atmosphere of the school was something that he preferred. He remembered that sending a child to boarding school had become for his family, "kind of a tradition":

> I guess you could say [chuckle] that the Indian kids went to the public school and sat at the back row, and if they took typing, and there wasn't enough typewriters, well, they got left out. Stuff like that. So that was probably another reason they liked to send them to Indian schools. Cause they was all Indians up there [chuckles].

The histories that Child recovers and this man's memories illustrate that although boarding schools certainly created problems by displacing students and severely restricting their freedom or by limiting life options for students after school, they also provided certain possibilities for students that would not have been available to them at other schools. One of these possibilities was the formation of intertribal alliances relatively free from outside racism and based upon common historical experiences of racial exclusion. This understanding of boarding school as a cultural resource is reflected in ideas and emotions expressed about sports at boarding schools during this period.

Sports were an important institution that the Collier administration set out to reform within the system of off-reservation boarding schools. After the Meriam Report, the BIA had begun to discourage boarding schools from using sports as a public relations tool, in large part because accusations of professionalism and corruption had created embarrassments for the BIA (Bloom 1996). In 1931, on the eve of Collier's reign over the BIA, officials in Washington had begun to draw a stark contrast between a collegiate-level athletic system that they saw as costly and exploitative and a high school–level athletic system that they saw as more in line with the goals of federal Indian educational policy. In a report to the BIA on athletics at the Albuquerque Indian School, Harold Bentley used the occasion to contrast what he saw as a favorable high school system at Albuquerque with a more corrupt system that existed at Haskell (*An Enquiry into the Status of Athletics and Physical Education: Albuquerque Indian School* 1931). Collier went even further, discouraging school sports teams altogether in favor of more participatory recreational activities. The 1941 *Manual for the Indian School Service*, for example, states that "[i]ntramural athletics and games in which everybody has a chance to play shall be encouraged, rather than formal gymnastics or calisthenics or interscholastic athletic competition" (Bureau of Indian Affairs 1941, 26).

The reforms initiated by the Collier administration, as well as the changes in boarding schools brought about because of the Meriam Report, seem to have had an effect on football programs, perhaps the most successful and highly visible sport at boarding schools between 1890 and 1930. Institutional changes, for example, that lowered the average age of boarding school students severely undercut the ability of highly visible teams to win against college competition. This transformation most dramatically affected the football team at Haskell. It went from being ranked number 4 among college teams by the Associated Press in 1927 to being dropped from the schedules of its most respected opponents by the mid-1930s because of its inability to field adequately competitive teams. Haskell eventually eliminated competition against college teams altogether by March 1939.

Many Haskell alumni were among the most vocal in their opposition to the elimination of a college schedule for the football team. In 1935, for example, George Shawnee, secretary of the Haskell Alumni Association, wrote to the acting superintendent of Haskell expressing concern over the football team's recent lack of success. The letter vaguely referred to "rumors" that the school might veer away from high-profile college athletics. Shawnee expressed concern over such a move, arguing that the football team had been an important, publicly visible symbol for Native American people around the United States. Referring to the massive fund-raising effort in the mid-1920s that helped build Haskell's 10,000-seat stadium with money entirely generated from indigenous people, Shawnee wrote,

> We know it could not have been accomplished without the splendid showing of the football team during those years and the widely accepted belief among the Indians that it was worthy of this extraordinary recognition. They believed the public looked upon the team as representing not only Haskell but the Indian race, and they wished to give to the school any equipment which might enable it to maintain its proud place in college athletics. (Shawnee 1935)

Shawnee associated the football team with Indian national pride, but an essential element of this association was football's success at obtaining national recognition for Native Americans. By the 1930s it had become well established that receiving national recognition required playing and beating college football teams, which Haskell was not doing when Shawnee wrote his letter and which the alumni he represented seem to have desired greatly. Former Carlisle football star Gus Welch had become the head coach at Haskell after the firing of the school's long-time coach and athletic director, Frank W. McDonald, in November 1932, and Shawnee blamed Welch for the team's losses:

Reasons may be given why the team has at times been badly defeated, why it has been dropped from the schedules of its old time friendly rivals, why gate receipts have fallen far below reasonable expectations, and the year closed with disastrous shortage of money, many unpaid bills, and a ruined credit, but the alumni feel it is the coach. We hear reports that your athletic funds are entirely exhausted and that it is impossible to obtain a loan. Wherever the fault lies for this unfortunate situation, they feel that the two years Mr. Welch has been coach and manager have served to demonstrate that he cannot succeed. This sentiment seems to prevail also down-town among many of Haskell's best friends and supporters, and we feel should be taken into account to secure their best co-operation. (Shawnee 1935)

Shawnee's letter suggests the symbolic importance that football represented for many who attended Haskell, but it is also evidence of the decreasing viability of football as a vehicle for the expression of Indian pride at boarding schools. Contrary to Shawnee's statement, the fortunes of the team began to decline under the reign of McDonald and had to do more with the changing population of the student body than with the abilities of the coach. By the early 1930s Haskell was no longer allowed to enroll students more than twenty-one years of age or to perpetually keep good football players enrolled by continually moving them from one vocational program to another after each had been completed. The relative youth and small size of football teams from Haskell put the team at a great disadvantage against even small-college competition during the 1930s. This was a problem not only at Haskell but also at other boarding schools, such as Chilocco in northern Oklahoma. The Chilocco graduate quoted earlier played football there, and he recalled during our interview (April 21, 1995) what it was like to play against college teams. He remembered that in the tenth grade, weighing only 150 pounds, he played both end and guard against small-college teams from southern Kansas:

[The opposition wasn't] big like they are now, but they were bigger than we were ... probably 180 pounders. Maybe some of them weighed 200....

We did pretty good with them. We'd win some games. And then we'd ...
but we were competitive with 'em.

As this man's recollections illustrate, even when losing, players
took great pride in how they competed, particularly when the odds were
against them.[3] By contrast, however, officials from the BIA expressed both
relief and support for the elimination of college competition. The break
from college athletics came in the spring of 1939, and it not only brought
Haskell down to the high school level, but it also involved the promotion
of more intramural sports. In a letter to G. Warren Spaulding, acting
superintendent of Haskell, the BIA director of education, Willard W.
Beatty, praised the school's administration for bringing the boarding
school into line with federal policy goals:

> May I express my hearty commendation to you and to Mr. Carmody
> [Haskell's director of physical education at the time] for your courage for
> finally breaking with the college athletic competition which has charac-
> terized the Haskell athletic set-up for a number of years. I appreciate that
> it has been difficult for Haskell students, alumni, and faculty to appreciate
> the change which has come about with regard to the characteristics of the
> male student body over the period of years which has elapsed since the
> great days of John Levi and other Indian athletic heroes. (Beatty 1939)

In his letter Beatty goes on to recognize the importance of produc-
ing a winning team for the school, in fact arguing that the lower level of
competition would help "your boys ... 'bring home the bacon.'" However,
he ends by pointing out, "I shall stand unwaveringly behind you regardless
of what happens, but I know as well as you do that a successful athletic season next year will aid in adjustment to the change which you have made."
This last sentence, which ends the letter, suggests that both the BIA and
the Haskell administration recognized sports as a highly valued component of boarding school life for many people connected with the school.

Perhaps one reason why Beatty was willing to concede the importance of a winning football team had to do with another athletic development during the 1930s at boarding schools. With the decline of football, a less expensive sport, one requiring fewer participants yet involving even greater levels of hypermasculine combat, began to rise in popularity to such a degree that it had become a core aspect of life at many boarding schools by the end of the decade: boxing. As one might also surmise, it was a sport that evoked even greater conflicts with the BIA. Yet its importance to students during this period illustrates the significance of pride and pan-Indian nationalism.

## Boxing and Native American Boarding Schools

In late October 1933 the BIA received an anonymous letter postmarked from Arkansas City, Kansas, expressing concern over the popularity of boxing at the Chilocco Indian School. The letter writer asserted that boxing was "made more than a school activity," that the school print shop was used to print publicity posters, and that revenue from the bouts might have been tampered with. The letter ends with a thinly veiled accusation: "Large crowds are always present and what becomes of the gate receipts?" (Anonymous Letter 1933).

The commissioner's office sent investigators to Chilocco in response to this letter. They uncovered no evidence of embezzlement, but the prominence of the boxing team did cause concern at the BIA. Its director of education, W. Carson Ryan, worried in a memo about professionalism creeping into boarding school athletics, and he asked if there was a need to review athletic policy at boarding schools. Two years later commissioner Collier, responding to an article published in an Oklahoma newspaper, voiced his criticism of boxing at the school. He wrote to Chilocco's superintendent, L. E. Correll, "Newspaper clippings and other information coming to this office relative to your boxing team would lead me to believe that perhaps you are over-emphasizing this sport" (Collier 1935).

Boxing began at Chilocco in 1932 when a sports promoter from Wichita, Kansas, persuaded Superintendent Correll to field a team from Chilocco for an American Legion tournament. Chilocco's team performed well even though it had been hastily trained. Only one year later, boxers from the school traveled to amateur tournaments as far away as Boston and were celebrated on the pages of *Ring* magazine (Bradfield 1963, 122–23).

Boxing was not popular only at Chilocco, although it undoubtedly had the best and most famous team. Other Indian boarding schools also created popular boxing teams during the 1930s. Teams from Albuquerque, Haskell, Phoenix, and Santa Fe were quite successful, sending boxers to regional and national AAU tournaments. Boarding schools fought against one another, but they also competed with local colleges, high schools, and amateur boxing clubs.

In a relatively short time, coincidental with a decline in the status of football, boxing emerged during the 1930s as one of the most important sports on Indian school campuses and as a prominent part of boarding school life. Institutional changes only partly explain why such a sport would grow in stature. Boxing was also a sport that resonated with the lives of boarding school students. Changes in federal policy, school funding, and economic climate all were important to introducing boxing to boarding schools, but students developed and made meaning of the sport as an important part of their cultural lives. For example, Lomawaima writes that violent play, fights, and gangs were common at Chilocco among the male students. She argues that such behavior was, in fact, an expression of a more pervasively violent culture of discipline and authority that existed at boarding school. She writes, "Fighting to settle differences was common, an accepted method of working things out. Not surprisingly, the boxers were foremost among Chilocco's athletic teams. They won Golden Glove status and traveled to fights in Chicago and Madison Square Garden" (1994, 112–13).

Oral history interviews that I conducted with former boarding school students support Lomawaima's observations. A Navajo man who fought for the Santa Fe Indian School during the 1930s recalled in a

February 20, 1995, interview with me that such an atmosphere motivated him to take up boxing. He remembered how the boys' adviser, a man named Stein, would beat the children with a strap for violating rules: "I used to think about the time when I grew up. I said, I'm going to be a fighter. I'm going to tangle with that Mr. Stein, the boys' adviser. But he left before then."

If male students readily took to boxing as it became introduced into the boarding school athletic curriculum, then it is also true that the symbols and structures of amateur boxing during the 1930s helped to shape the kind of cultural expressions students would make through the sport. As Lomawaima indicates in her discussion of Chilocco's boxing team, boarding school fighters often competed at national amateur tournaments sponsored by the AAU. In oral history interviews, former fighters and boarding school students often highlighted these events, even more than they did boxing matches that took place between boarding schools. AAU tournaments usually took place in big cities. They began with elimination matches in places such as Albuquerque or Wichita, and winners advanced first to a more general set of regional bouts in Kansas City or Denver and ultimately to a national gathering in Chicago, New York, or Boston. The results of these fights received national attention in newspapers. This particular structure of amateur boxing in the United States during the 1930s made the sport a particularly meaningful one, for it offered fighters an opportunity to get off campuses within which many former students often report feeling isolated. Fighters I interviewed told of the excitement they experienced performing upon a public stage at AAU tournaments. The Navajo man previously quoted, for example, told me of his experience fighting at an AAU tournament held in Chicago Stadium during the 1930s:

> It looked like Chicago was almost spending full time in the gymnasium hoping to ... to ... boys and men that were interested in boxing because they had one, two, three, four rings going all at one time.
> BLOOM: Wow. And a lot of people watching.
> A lot of people watching, yeah ... I think it is a big stadium there.

For some, such national tournaments provided a forum in which they could express a strong sense of pride. Within the sport of amateur boxing, this pride was often understood in terms of race. The urban contexts of AAU tournaments tended to blur together distinctions within groups, and fighters were often categorized within broadly defined terms of national identity. For example, when I asked this man what ethnic groups those he fought belonged to, he replied, "The majority I think were black, with here and there Caucasians and very few Spanish." A different Navajo man, who also fought for the Santa Fe Indian School during the 1930s expressed a sense of racial combat more explicitly. When I asked him, in an interview on January 13, 1995, why he was a successful fighter, he replied,

> I fought many a different people, like Anglo people, black people, you know, and boy, I'm telling you, you put me in the ... put my gloves on, I know for what I'm doing. You got the pride ... if there's any race that's speaking different languages you got the pride to demonstrate that you going to be in there fighting ... because you're an Indian, you going to show what an Indian can do. So that was always my intention, 'cause when I fought against a black, man, well ... I fought.

Both Elliott Gorn and Jeffrey Sammons have written about the important symbolism that national and racial pride have had in professional prizefighting. The idea that a fighter is a representative of one's race is a deep thread running through the history of boxing in the United States (see Gorn 1986; Sammons 1988). Such ideas were also a part of the amateur boxing culture of the 1930s and early 1940s. One particularly ironic example appeared in the February 13, 1941, edition of the *Santa Fe New Mexican*, whose article "Indian Meets Denver Negro" reported that a "negro from Denver" and an "O'jibway Indian" would meet for the "'white hope' trophy offered the heavyweight champion in the Rocky Mountain AAU Regional boxing tournament."

At the same time, this kind of racial discourse surrounding boxing resonated with historically particular aspects of the boarding school life that students experienced, especially the ideological contradictions that were an inherent aspect of the assimilation task assigned to these institutions. The very notion of assimilation that had guided boarding school policies from their beginning had tended to connote the erasure of European ethnicity that would allow immigrants and their children a common privilege of white racial identity in U.S. culture. Yet boarding schools, in their very definition of "Indian," constructed Native Americans as a "racial" category. Entry qualifications at schools had little to do with cultural background. Instead, they were based upon blood quantum. In this manner, boarding schools simultaneously forced assimilation while denying its possibility. This contradiction characterized the earliest uses of athletics at Carlisle and Haskell. Their teams provided schools with a visible public identity that validated the government-run boarding school mission for white audiences. Football and track teams that competed successfully allowed boarding school advocates to show that Indians could be successfully "Americanized." At the same time, sports drew heightened attention to the players themselves as biologically defined racial "others" (Churchill, Hill, and Barlow 1979; Malmsheimer 1985).

Amateur boxing during the 1930s provided a stage upon which boarding school students could appropriate racial identities as a source of pride. However, this is not necessarily to say that it erased cultural differences among students. As Lomawaima points out, students at Chilocco were very conscious of their tribal languages and identities. In addition, they divided themselves along a variety of other lines, including race (all students, she writes, were aware of those who had African lineage), geographical origin, gender, religion, age, vocation, and even athletic skill (1994, 125). In fact, the Navajo man of my January 13 interview, who was previously quoted as framing his own involvement in boxing in terms of racial pride, also associated prowess in different sports with particular tribal identities. He drifted into this discussion during our interview after I asked if he was ever allowed to speak his native language at school:

> Different tribes of Indians came to school here, and any number of, say like over twenty different-speaking Indians, languages are spoken here that

represent different, from different parts of the United States. So that's what they were. Why they have, some are interested in playing basketball … well, they used to have a basketball team, they travel different places, you know. And they play good teams.… And then again there are these track teams at, some of those Indians, oooh my. They get some of the fastest runners. You know, like, they have, uh, the state record. There was, uh, that would represent them, like, uh, Kia Begay, no Key Begay.… He was a Navajo. He was a fine runner. Nobody could beat that man.

Historian Joe Sando, a Santa Fe Indian School graduate, echoed this relationship between athletic skill and tribal origin during an interview I conducted with him on January 10, 1995. He told me, "I guess some of the basketball players came from South Dakota because they were taller and there were mixed breeds." These testimonials suggest that boxing provided a context for the prideful expression of pan-Indian identities among boarding school students, expressions that were made possible because of the particular circumstances that surrounded amateur fighting during the 1930s. However, such interview responses also suggest that such expressions coexisted alongside a continued awareness of diversity among students and did not necessarily represent a stage within a linear process of assimilation.

The BIA opposed boxing and banned it in 1948, as Chapter 4 discusses in greater depth. However, during the 1930s it also took a greater interest in the expression of Native American identity at boarding schools, and it even promoted expressions of pride. At boarding schools and in Native American communities, this new attitude took a number of different forms. At the Santa Fe Indian School, for example, art educator Dorothy Dunn began an Indian arts program in which students were encouraged to explore their histories through traditional expressions, such as pottery and weaving, as well as through other artistic forms, such as painting (Hyer 1990). Narciso Abeyta, the well-known Navajo painter (and, incidently, Golden Gloves boxer) was but one student who was able to take advantage of this and build an art career upon his education.

Yet it is important to keep in mind the conservative implications of many such programs when considering the popularity and problems that boxing generated during this decade. Before the Meriam Report, boarding school administrators tended to favor a strict assimilationist approach to education, in large part cutting students off completely from their ethnic traditions and cultural memories. Although programs such as the Indian arts school at Santa Fe contrast with this approach, they also attempted to recuperate Native American traditions in the service of a progressive set of assimilationist goals. In other words, whereas boarding schools had been built at the turn of the century to assimilate Native American children by eradicating their memory of Native American ethnicity and history, federal policy during the 1930s attempted to use cultural memory to enlist and legitimate a nationalist ideology.

An example of this is the Gallup Indian Ceremonial held in August 1938. The ceremonial consisted of exhibits featuring "authentic Indian-made goods" from the southwestern Pueblos, goods that the BIA had encouraged Indians to develop into marketable products. The agency's monthly magazine, *Indians at Work*, featured a photo of one such exhibit that illustrated the uses of such items in the decor of the "modern home." This represents a significant change from earlier policies, which positioned Native American culture and traditions as incompatible with middle-class norms and values. In this case, the Indian Ceremonial presented Pueblo arts and traditions as entirely compatible with middle-class tastes, commodity buying, and family living. The BIA seemed to be enlisting one form of Native American cultural memory to establish federal leadership and commodity capitalism as legitimate markers of progress, as represented by the "modern home" ("Pueblo Art in the Modern Home" 1939).

George Lipsitz has argued that within popular culture, ethnic memories have often been used to establish the legitimacy of new social arrangements built around consumption, making individualistic acquisition and consumption seem consistent with "traditional values." Yet he also argues that evoking such memory invites counterinterpretations of the present drawn from the textured experiences of the past. There is always the potential that drawing from memory might not transform values, that they might instead recall a past that can be used to understand the present and future critically rather than ahistorically (Lipsitz 1990 39–75). Although the BIA was ultimately conservative in the way it encouraged expressions of ethnic memory, such memories created the possibility for critically understanding the present. For example, the Indian arts program at the Santa Fe Indian School would in 1962 become the Institute for American Indian Arts in Santa Fe, a training ground for a number of Native American artists who would provide a strong critical vision of contemporary Native American life in the United States by drawing upon the experiences of indigenous peoples in the Americas (Shutes and Mellick 1996).

Boxing helped to forge new ethnic identities for Native American boarding school students. However, it was a sport that was also seemingly at odds with federal aims to direct the cultural life of students toward productive ends, at the very time that the BIA was allowing students to express themselves as ethnically connected to diverse and historically significant nations. The huge popularity of the sport among students, as well as its strong association with pride rooted in the common historic experiences of Native American people, suggest that for some, boxing made it possible to understand expressions of cultural memory in diverse ways.[4]

Collier's early criticism of boxing is somewhat typical of other elitist criticisms of sports and popular culture as nonproductive and nonserious. Perhaps at stake with the passions boxing evoked, however, were some very serious issues regarding the ways in which Native Americans would draw upon shared memories and identities to challenge their social positions in the future. The popular appeal of boxing matches drew upon historical memory and identity. Combat in the ring, though violent and brutal, graphically symbolized common bonds of identity and pride.

Both football and boxing, however, were also highly masculine forms of sports competition. If one is to understand the pride created by such athletic contests in any depth, it is important to think critically about the points of view not represented by displays of national pride through violent, combative, male-dominated sports. In a documentary on the

Santa Fe Indian School made during the 1980s, a woman who attended the school during the 1930s recalled boxing matches with a tinge of ambivalence that is very revealing. She said, "I never really thought I'd like boxing, but I really enjoyed it then" (Reyna et al. 1987). In fact, as Marlon Riggs and Renee Tajima-Pena have explored in their documentary film explorations of ethnicity, race, and identity, the empowerment that a cohesive sense of national identity might provide has another edge to it. It can often make those identified within a particular category feel as if they must subsume intra-ethnic differences for the good of the common group.

The statement "I never really thought I'd like boxing, but I really enjoyed it then" is important and complex. On one hand, boxing is a brutal sport that elevates violence and masculine body power in ways that translate to real oppressions faced by women at the hands of men. This is more than an abstract notion. As Lomawaima (1994) describes, boxing reflected a very real atmosphere of physical violence and intimidation that existed among boys at boarding schools.

At the same time, the quotation locates the enjoyment of boxing at a particular moment in time, one that corresponds with her own life course, as well as with a significant time historically ("I really enjoyed it then"). Although in the video she does not specifically discuss her own enjoyment of boxing in terms of national pride, her own contextualization of boarding school boxing and its meaning is important. Along with her many comments that do overtly discuss the importance of pride, this comment suggests that sports were a significant part of a dynamic understanding of ethnicity among Native Americans at boarding schools during the twentieth century, and specifically during the 1930s.

Boarding school alumni whom I interviewed sometimes told me in informal conversations that the BIA eventually banned boxing in 1948 because a fighter had either been killed or seriously injured in the ring. I could not find any evidence to support this claim, but, curiously, the official statement announcing the ban did include a discussion of the crowds that tend to watch boxing matches and the dangerous passions that the matches seemed to arouse in their audiences. In an article published in *Indian Education* announcing the ban, the BIA director of health, Fred Foard, and the agency director of education, Willard W. Beatty, wrote,

> There is still an animal-like ferocity in many of us, which accounts for attendance at prize fights, wrestling matches, midget auto races and other spectacles where life is endangered or where sadistic punishment is inflicted. (Foard and Beatty 1948)

Whether or not anyone was ever seriously hurt in the boxing ring, the statement by the BIA, and particularly its focus on the crowd, suggests that the battle over boxing was in part a battle over leisure time, and it was not only a battle that the BIA fought with students. The crowds that attended boxing matches were a source of revenue for promoters and a financial and public relations opportunity for school administrators. Because of such contradictory motives and imperatives, boxing flourished at boarding schools between 1931 and 1948. Students often found within the sport a tremendous source of pleasure and excitement and a context in which they could claim their leisure time for their own.

It is ironic that sports were instituted as a mechanism for the promotion of moral character, for in the case of boxing, their practice could also offend the moral sensibilities of those who operated boarding schools. Boxing matches were exciting events where students who generally felt cooped up all week on campus could interact with a variety of people; where they could see their matrons, teachers, and superintendents yelling and cheering; or where they could simply socialize. At Chilocco, boxing matches were especially exciting events, drawing both students and people from around the region. A man who attended the school during the 1930s recalled in an April 21, 1995, interview, that

> [a]t Chilocco, the people would come from miles around for that boxing. There's something about it, about boxing. It's kind of like gambling I guess, people were *crazy* about it! Boy, they just packed that gym. Just packed it up.... It was just those ranchers from over around Powhuska, and people

from Wichita, Kansas, and people from Tulsa would come up for it. That's a hundred miles, you know. Back then, that was about a three- or four-hour drive. But they'd come up there and just pack that gym.

A student quoted by Sally Hyer in her history of the Santa Fe Indian School recalled a similar atmosphere in that institution's gymnasium for a fight:

I didn't get knocked out, but I got knocked down once. That was in the state championship when we were playing. I was fighting a Spanish guy from El Rito about six inches taller than me. We had the championship here at the gym. People came from all over the state. It was kind of scary.... We made it, all right. We got the state [championship]!" (Hyer 1990, 52)

Students and townspeople were not the only ones caught up in the fever of a boxing match. Students remember school staff also becoming excited at these events. A husband and wife who attended Santa Fe Indian School, interviewed by Santa Fe student Geoffrey Kellogg (Sioux), Sally Hyer, and Frank Tenorio (San Felipe) as part of a 100-year school anniversary oral history project in 1986, recalled how teachers and superintendents enjoyed boxing matches:

HUSBAND: [The school Doctor] would take in every game. And we'd have boxing matches, he'd be there. One of the biggest fans we had was [female teacher]. Remember her? She always bought a seat. Just as you went in the door, here would be the boxing ring. She would sit right here on the right side. And [student fighter] was her pet. "Come on, ... throw the left, throw the right! Hit him with ———! [Laughing heartily] She'd stand up, you know.
WIFE: Like she was going through the motions, you know.
HYER: Was she hospital staff?
HUSBAND: No, she was a English teacher! [Laughs] (First One Hundred Years Oral History Project [*Santa Fe Indian School*] [hereafter *First One Hundred Years*], May 14, 1986)

These descriptions of boxing matches are themselves an important part of boarding school folklore. They illustrate moments when student life broke from the monotony of daily routine, when students were able to interact with society outside the walls of the campus, and when they could observe their teachers acting in ways that they had not seen. Ultimately, they illustrate how important leisure time, pleasure, and pride were to students, how play and fun were actually part of a larger struggle to carve out their own lives.

## Re-reading Native American Identity through Boarding School Sports

In his insightful book on running among Native Americans, Peter Nabokov writes about a 375-mile run by young Pueblo Indians in August 1980 from Taos, New Mexico, to Second Mesa, Arizona. The runners were retracing the footsteps of a famous courier mission that had taken place 300 years earlier, a mission that had helped to ignite Pope's rebellion of the Pueblo Indians against colonists from Spain, "the most successful Indian rebellion in American History" (Nabokov 1981, 9). Throughout the text, he weaves descriptions of running in Native American history, folklore, and religion into his own journalistic accounts of this event. He pays particular attention to the complexity of running as a cultural expression that is common to many Native American tribes and peoples and that yet is employed in enormously diverse ways as well.

Toward the end of the book, Nabokov writes about Indian runners competing in "the White Man's Arena." He notes the long history, dating back to the sixteenth century, of whites placing Native American athletes on display for their amusement, and he discusses the trials and difficulties that indigenous runners have had in bringing an athletic form associated with deep-seated cultural traditions and histories into a sporting context organized around entertainment, exploitation, and commerce. Nabokov tells the poignant story of Carlisle distance runner Louis Tewanima, a Hopi from the Sand Clan who some said would run "the 120 miles from home to Winslow [Arizona] and back, barefoot, just to watch the trains pass" (179). As noted in chapter 1, Tewanima became a very successful runner at Carlisle, earning silver medals in the 5,000- and 10,000-meter races in the 1912 Olympic games in Stockholm, Sweden. Nabokov, however, also writes that Tewanima was less successful as a runner after returning home:

> According to Fred Kabotie, his performance at a home-state race seemed almost a contest between native and white styles of training ... "We were in the Winslow grandstand and there was Louis, and about three other Hopi runners, not Carlisle students, and Zuni runners with animal fetishes to give them strength which they held the entire race. When they started Louis was out in front by a long stretch. About the third round, the Hopi runners passed him up, then the Zunis passed him up. He didn't even finish. It turned out Pop Warner's training didn't do any good against those Hopi runners." (182)

This account is largely about the pain created by the loss of memory that took place at federal Indian boarding schools. Its author, Fred Kabotie, is careful to note how those competing against Tewanima wore "animal fetishes" and were rooted in local tradition. The final sentence about Pop Warner seems to say that although the white coach (and by extension white society) might get credit for the success of Indian runners, Hopi and Zuni cultures, largely unrecognized by dominant society, are far more powerful.

Yet Kabotie's account is also somewhat misleading. It positions Tewanima as a purely assimilated Indian competing against seemingly static traditions that he had abandoned. Yet for many, by the 1930s boarding schools had become an important part of what it meant to be a Native American. Although boarding schools and white coaches undoubtedly exploited such local Native American traditions as running, it is important not to discount the extent to which athletic traditions became a meaningful part of how new national identities could become expressed.

A man who had boxed for Santa Fe, for example, discussed with me how he gained from boxing a strong sense of self-confidence. In a February 20, 1995, interview, he recalled that after a fight, other students would say about him, "He's got grace and dignity, endurance, and that type of thing." It is precisely these things that he said he learned through running as a Navajo child before he went off to boarding school at age six:

> We were under the care of the medicine man, my uncle. . . . A loud singer. And he would get us up in the morning and we'd rub snow on arms or thighs, bathe in the snow. Then we'd get our blood circulating. We had a truck field, and around we'd go. Then we'd build a great big fire and get warmed up, get clothes on. Toughening up situation, that's what it was.

This man's experiences and traditions associated with Navajo running were not directly translated into his boarding school sports experiences. However, they were in dialogue with his athletic life at school. Running helped him prepare for fights and, as he stated, "take the fear out of your system." Confidence is also something that Native American audiences gained from sports, from the collective sense of victory that boarding school athletic contests provided. Employing a tradition like running in a boarding school athletic program might be seen as a debasement, fragmenting a cultural form from the contexts in which it was originally meaningful. Yet it might also be seen as creating new possibilities, as allowing students to survive another day as Native Americans in a hostile environment, and as constituting a precious resource from the past that allowed students to critically understand their present circumstances.

The entire course of boarding school history up to the 1930s presented concrete historical experiences that relate to the configuration of pan-Indian identities. From their earliest inception, boarding schools tended to blend tribes and nations in one school, making it harder for students to speak their own languages and fostering the learning of English. Although each Native American group might have had unique stories, traditions, languages, and histories, they also shared many common experiences: consolidation on reservations, removals, boarding school education, and general relations with an Anglo-European government. The Haskell homecoming seems to suggest that by 1926 sports had become a powerful and important vehicle for many diverse Native American groups to express pride in this new identity. Yet until the reforms that followed the Meriam Report, such pride could only be expressed in ways that were either covert or greatly disguised.

The 1930s—with the relaxation of inhibitions that had been placed upon students, with the increasing numbers of students attending boarding school, and with the more general social crisis caused by the Great Depression—represents a time of creative possibility. Pride was not only allowed, it was sometimes even encouraged within programs like the Indian arts school at Santa Fe. As George Lipsitz has argued, popular culture is a powerful aspect of cultural life. Subjugated groups draw from it to express pride through recollection of alternative memories from the past that exist in dialogue with concrete conditions in the present. Popular culture is a kind of hybrid of many different cultural forms and histories. It draws from diverse cultural memories and can be used creatively to represent hopes for the future (Lipsitz 1990).

CHAPTER 4

# Female Physical Fitness, Sexuality, and Pleasure

During a set of interviews I conducted with Navajo women who attended Indian boarding schools, I learned, somewhat predictably, that girls who attended these institutions did not have as many opportunities to participate in sports as boys. This was no surprise because between 1930 and 1973 it was generally the practice in U. S. schools to offer women very few chances to play on athletic teams or to play competitively (Cahn 1993). When I asked the two women (in separate interviews) why they were not able to play on teams, I expected them to say that school administrators would not allow females the same opportunities as males. I was surprised by their answers, for both said it was because Navajo parents and grandparents refused to let their daughters wear short pants in public.

A woman who attended Thoreau Indian School in western New Mexico during the 1950s discussed this with me in an interview on February 20, 1995. Rather than understanding the Navajo rules against females wearing shorts as a restriction, she felt that the boarding school requirement that she wear them was an infringement on her identity:

> With our tradition, we asked to have respect for each other if we were brother and sister as we grew up. And, um, we couldn't wear cutoffs, or we couldn't wear anything, even above our knees, or anything like that. So when we were sent off to the boarding school, we were actually embarrassed toward the boys. We didn't even wear anything that would go any

lower than this [gesture toward her knees]. And we were embarrassed toward the guys.

Unlike in the 1930s, during the 1950s boarding schools returned to a strict assimilationist curriculum, ordering students to wear uniforms and speak only English. This woman's father had sent her to boarding school because of economic hardship at home. He felt that learning English and skills like typing could help her live a more prosperous life. Yet she found the discipline that she faced at Thoreau extremely oppressive, involving severe punishments such as hard labor and ridicule. Her identity as a Navajo, which the boarding school curriculum was designed to teach her to repress, also provided her a position from which to criticize her education:

> They taught how to do ... setting the table up, how to eat, and put our arms out on one side, and always onto the manners.... We were totally told what to do. And some of us fought back. Some of us didn't want to have nothing to do with learning what's going on with the white man's world.

Another woman, who had attended nearby Ft. Wingate Indian School, also during the 1950s (whom I interviewed on January 11, 1995), likewise remembered Navajo resistance toward girls' wearing short pants. However, unlike the woman who went to Thoreau, she did not recall this as an act of rebellion. Rather, she saw it as an impediment to her ability to enjoy sports: "A lot of them still had their culture because our grandparents frowned upon for me to wearing shorts and short skirts.... As time when on, you know, with these new parents, all that changed." She wished she could have played sports and was unsatisfied with the physical education classes that girls received at school: "We did have PE, and we were required to take part. But the only [thing we] did was just run around." Although not allowed to play on teams, she did play in and help to organize baseball games on Sundays in the school commons: "It was not really sponsored by anyone. It was just done by the students themselves.... None of the adults was really in charge."

These memories comprise a complex set of interpretations. On one hand, each might be understood as "conservative" responses to boarding school life. The first woman seems to embrace female modesty, something that often aligns national pride with patriarchy. However, her discussion of "respect" for "one another" among Navajo boys and girls also must be understood within the context of the high level of gender equality within Navajo traditions. Navajo kinship is generally passed through females, providing women with a significant degree of power and authority. Because of this, it is difficult to interpret such a statement as a clear expression of Victorian patriarchal norms. It is much clearer, however, that her refusal to wear short pants provided her with a way to express pride in traditions that were denigrated at boarding schools and a way to use this pride to interpret the discipline she faced as a student as unfair and unjust.

The second woman's discussion might be seen as expressing an acceptance of assimilation. Unlike the first woman, she is critical of a Navajo tradition and presents it as a barrier to women's ability to advance and participate in athletics. In fact, in this matter one might view sports as actually serving as a wedge dividing Navajos. This, I would argue, would greatly oversimplify her story, for if examined carefully, it reveals something extremely important about sports at boarding schools, something as important as the national pride that athletic success evoked.

Like the first woman, the second remembered boarding school as a lonely, isolating experience away from home. She discussed the importance of making friends and the creation of a social life at boarding school:

> I didn't live too far from here, but still, not being home and being among strange students, especially at the beginning of the school year, and being in strange buildings made me homesick. But then as time get, goes on you get used to the place, and you get used to students and you make friends and before you know it feels right at home.

For her, sports, even attending the boys' sporting events as a member of the cheerleading squad, were an important part of this social life.

It was a time when students could get together to have fun, mingle, and socialize:

> I remember my first experience at boarding school was that it was very strict. Like the boys and girls couldn't mingle. We have our own boundary line. Like we have a cafeteria here, between the boys' and girls' residential halls, there was a cafeteria there, and no girl was allowed beyond this one certain line, and if you did you were punished for it. And the same way with the boys. And our discipline was very strict.... Back in those days I know it was considered that the BIA schools were run like a military.

As much as sports served as an expression of national, pan-Indian pride for students, they were equally important as sources of pleasure, fun, and desire. Whether the girls were excluded from sports because of school regulations or because of Navajo tradition did not matter much to the woman who had attended Ft. Wingate. Both meant that she had been denied an important resource for expressions of pleasure within a context where the most important lessons taught were discipline and the suppression of desire.

## Gender, Discipline, and Boarding School Sports

Navajo parents who objected to females wearing short pants were not the only ones who hindered girls from participating in sports. In fact, the orientation of boarding school curricula around gender ideologies that directed females toward domestic roles was probably the most crucial factor in limiting opportunities in athletics for girls. Women at boarding schools were primarily trained for duties such as sewing, taking care of a home, and raising children. From their founding, boarding schools focused an extraordinary amount of effort on women, training them less for employment than for roles as moral leaders in a domestic sphere.

For example, the *Annual Report for the Santa Fe Indian School* for 1911 gave the following description of its curriculum for female students:

> The girls of the school are taught those duties that will be useful to them later as housewives. Sewing, including cutting and fitting garments, darning

and repair work. Laundry work, ironing, general housework, nursing and the general care of the sick, and last but not least, family cooking, which is taught in our domestic science department, and is looked upon by many as our most valuable branch of industrial training for girls. (*Annual Report for the Santa Fe Indian School* 1911)

This emphasis upon domestic skills and ideology remained a core part of most boarding school curricula, even after the changes that took place during the 1930s and 1940s. The primary occupations listed in the Haskell curriculum for 1940/41 for girls, for example, were home economics, secretarial work, and child care. An entire section of the curriculum, titled "Social and Personal Development," was directed entirely at female students. Under this category of courses, girls took classes in Hygiene and Family Relationships that were intended to prepare them for their domestic roles. Under Hygiene, the school bulletin reads,

This course purports to give the student a clear understanding of the relationship of good health to attractiveness and success, to show her the responsibility she must accept in helping her family to realize good health habits, and to train her in the care of the sick and to give her a knowledge of simple first aid methods. (*Information Bulletin [Haskell]* 1940/41, 59)

Similarly, the course titled Family Relationships promised to instruct female students in

correct family relationships from the standpoint of individual development and adjustment in the home. The traits which go to make up good family citizenship are studied. The emphasis falls on the girl's responsibilities and duties in creating a happy home of her own after her marriage. (*Information Bulletin [Haskell]* 1940/41, 59–60)

Lomawaima writes, "To construct the ideal woman, educators had to teach Indian girls new identities, new skills and practices, new forms of appearance, and new physical mannerisms. Dormitory personnel, matrons and disciplinarians, academic teachers and trades instructors, all enforced a rigid code of appearance for Chilocco students" (1993, 231–32). Physical education for female students was a core aspect of this construction of an ideal woman. Documents left by school officials reveal that they thought a great deal about girls' physical training and that they thought of this aspect of the curriculum as central to lessons about behavior, sexuality, and discipline.

Female physical education heavily emphasized exercises and gymnastic drilling oriented toward this education in new identity. It placed less emphasis on competitive sports and athletics. Although girls did play intramural sports, and occasionally played interscholastic sports, the overwhelming emphasis of girls' physical activity focused upon the kind of bodily discipline that Lomawaima mentions. The Chilocco annual report for 1937, for example, makes only a passing reference to the intramural sports provided for girls. It begins by noting that each girl in the school is checked at the beginning of the school year, and each month after that, for height, weight, posture, motor ability, and "physical defects." The report includes a profile photograph, shot outside on the school grounds, of a girl standing upright, feet together, arms to each side. The photograph's caption states, "The best posture in the school—as a senior. As a freshie—was graded (D-) had flat feet and bad postural defects—Both were corrected by corrective exercise plus perserverance [sic] and pride in personal appearance" (*Annual Report for Chilocco Indian School* 1937, reel 19).

Such attention to the posture and bodily development of students, in the form of checklists and graded posture, exemplifies what Lomawaima describes as the surveillance that was central to the school's curricula. From the earliest years of federal Indian boarding schools, surveillance comprised a core part of student life, so much so that "it dwarfed any possible requirements of straightforward education" (Lomawaima 1993, 229). This was indicative of the larger role that boarding schools played—namely, to teach students to identify with the rules and imperatives of a modern institution, to behave as good matrons and good workers, and to repress one's desires.

The physical education curriculum mentioned in the report exemplifies this orientation toward bodily discipline. Girls took part in a variety of regular exercises, including parallel bars, Swedish horse, balance beams, swinging rings, club swinging, marching, tumbling and stunts, gymnastics, acrobatics, ballroom dancing, folk dancing, and ballet. Games such as basketball, volleyball, baseball, and tennis are listed as "High Organized Games." They are only discussed in brief as sports "that are given so that girls may learn team play and develop a better all around sportsmanship." There is also an account of a play day that took place on May 1, 1937, at Southwestern College in Winfield, Kansas, where girls played a variety of sports, including baseball, track, basketball, volleyball, Ping-Pong, marbles, jacks, bean bag games, and checkers.

Ideologically, this curriculum is meaningful for its relationship to issues of race and sexuality. The emphasis on physical appearance, posture, and body control for females is something that, as Susan Cahn has noted, was common in educational institutions throughout the United States during the early half of the twentieth century, particularly after the early 1930s. It reflected larger concerns over female morality and the control of female sexuality. According to Lomawaima, these issues were even more exaggerated at boarding schools because of a "deep-seated, racially defined perception of Indian people's physical bodies as 'uncivilized'" (Lomawaima 1993, 229). The Chilocco annual report expresses the hope that physical education might teach self-control as an internalized component of play, which was defined as the portion of the day when students were not supervised. It concludes with a statement that girls' physical education is of benefit to female students "so that they may continue to care for their minds ... and bodies after they leave school, and make intelligent use of their leisure time."

The report ends with a particularly intriguing passage on what its author terms "mental hygiene":

I have come to the conclusion that discoveries in branches of endocrinology should be applied to the work of physiology, hygiene, and physical education. They, the glands, are responsible for varied illnesses, ailments, and peculiarities that have been otherwise unexplained. . . . I asked cooperation of all the teacher's [*sic*] in all the academic department [*sic*] in detecting and listing of students who might be gland suspects. As a result of my research, together with responses of two or three of the teachers, I turned in a list to Mr. Correll, the superintendent. It seems that most of the few problem cases may be explained, studied, and corrected through this channel, and in my department, detected more readily than anywhere else. (*Annual Report for Chilocco Indian School* 1937)

This section is somewhat cryptic in how it defines a "gland suspect." However, its discussion of endocrinology suggests that it refers to female hormones, which had just been discovered in the 1920s. Under the heading of "Mental Hygiene," it defines sexuality among female students as unclean, sick, and in need of being controlled. This paragraph reveals the active role taken by physical educators at Chilocco (and other boarding schools) in the surveillance and control of female sexual desire. This control was so tightly monitored, according Brenda Child, that girls housed in dormitories had their windows nailed shut and fire escapes locked. This created a serious fire hazard for those sleeping inside, but it was seen as a legitimate act: "[B]ecause of the fear that boys would pay nocturnal visits to the girls' rooms, safety was given secondary consideration" (Child 1993, 106).

On a less dramatic level, girls and boys constantly received messages on self-control in their leisure time. Federal policy makers and educators at boarding schools during the 1930s relaxed rules governing student time a great deal, leaving students with far more time to themselves than they had had in previous decades. However, they were particularly concerned that this time be used "productively." This concern can be seen in artifacts left behind by boarding schools. In the 1930s, for example, the student-run newspaper at Chilocco Indian School, the *Indian School Journal*, contained numerous articles advising students on how to behave during their leisure time. An article from January 6, 1939, for example, advises that "leisure time is your own time to do anything you wish," and goes on to assert that "your leisure time should be spent in doing something that will help you some day." Another article from November 5, 1937, advises students on how to select a good movie, and another, from November 11, 1938, advises students to be quiet when watching a movie or a play. A blurb in a December, 3, 1937, edition warns students about the "evil effect" that a "lazy person" has upon a workplace.

Although these articles were presumably written by students, they at the very least indicate moral lessons that students were learning in the classroom and that they would have projected within a campus publication. Student assemblies and plays at Chilocco also reflected lessons in leisure-time behavior. In particular, they addressed relationships between the sexes and stressed proper manners, etiquette, and sexual restraint. The annual report for Chilocco for the year 1936 lists assemblies with titles such as "Gracious Living," "Straight Thinking," "The Girl Boys Admire," and "The Kind of Boy Girls Like" (*Annual Report for Chilocco Indian School* 1936).

The script for "The Kind of Boy Girls Like" consists of a conversation between two female Chilocco students, Ruby and Welta. After reflecting upon a school newspaper article written by a boy on the kind of girls that boys admire, the two make a list of characteristics of their own for the opposite sex. Ruby begins by saying, "I like a boy who is clean—clean in every way—thought and speech, too." She goes on to note that "the boy who knows how to treat me is sure to make a hit with me." The conversation ends by associating sports with such strong moral character traits.

> RUBY: I should say that a boy who is a real sport is sure to register.
> WELTA: Sure, and I'll put down something about the boy who does things well. Notice how the football or boxing hero is always found on the list of "Who's who"? (*Annual Report for Chilocco Indian School* 1936)

Campus sketches and assemblies that students put on in 1937 also reflect similar themes. Each has a moral, and many are directed at girls. One, for example, states, "If you want to be liked by the boys, make yourself liked by the girls first." Another states, "Any girl can 'neck,' but it's a clever girl who doesn't have to in order to get along" (*Annual Report for Chilocco Indian School* 1937).

These sketches, as well as the report from the physical education program at Chilocco, convey the basic assumption that sexual desire is not a component of preferred female behavior. The physical education report uses a language of psychological contamination ("mental hygiene") to describe feelings of sexual desire for females and of criminality ("gland suspects") to describe female students who are interested in sex. The skits portray "normal" females as those attracted to boys who can control their sexual desire, and they describe the fulfillment of sexual pleasure (in the form of "necking") as a duty that some young women might feel they have to fulfill rather than as something they might do for their own enjoyment. These texts illustrate an intense attention to the control of female sexuality, particularly within the sphere of their leisure time.

Lomawaima understands this attention to the sexuality of young women at boarding schools as not only being related to gender but also as reflecting ideologies connected to socially constructed racial categories. She writes that such policies were linked to "racially defined perceptions" of Native American bodies. To the boarding schools' earliest founders, Native American women were physically too strong and too well adapted to the outdoors. In fact, examples of females working in outdoor settings were sometimes used as evidence of how indigenous women were abused. This attitude toward proper female physical activity led to a severe neglect of even the most basic recreational equipment for girls at schools. The following statement by the superintendent of the Santa Fe Indian School, B. L. Smith, in his annual report for 1926, reflects this disregard for girls' recreation and athletics, as well as the association of physical activity among women with mental "breakdown":

> With the exception of football and baseball, the girls have the same chance as the boys [at sports]. But we are trying the experiment of keeping the girls off the more vigorous forms of athletic exercise. The more I see of that among girls and women, the more I am convinced that it is harmful. Our

girls are given eight to ten minutes of calisthenics before breakfast. That is most excellent, and unless I am badly mistaken (and I don't think I am), that is enough for the day, especially when we take into consideration the other activities that the girls engage in in the course of the day which require muscular exercise. We have, temporarily at least, discontinued basket-ball for girls; volley ball—they simply will not play it (and I can't blame them much, for it is pretty inane); dancing they like. And nearly every evening, the girls dance in their assembly room at their building for half an hour or so. And with that program during the past year, we had fewer breakdowns among our girls than for some time past. (*Annual Report for the Santa Fe Indian School* 1926)

In oral history interviews, former female students remember the limitations placed on girls when it came to playing sports, and the central role of drills, exercises, and other activities in their physical education. A woman interviewed by Sally Hyer who attended Santa Fe Indian School in the late 1910s and early 1920s remembered that the school offered girls

[b]aseball, basketball. But the girls weren't allowed to play basketball at one time, because one of the girls broke her arm. And they quit letting the girls play basketball for a while. Then running and drilling. Drilling is about the most we did! (Laughs) And dancing, of course; we danced quite a bit in our own girls' building.
HYER: Like ballroom dancing?
Yeah, girls dance with girls. (*First One Hundred Years*, May 28, 1986)[1]

This quotation illustrates how one student experienced the implementation of the girls' physical education program noted earlier. During the 1930s, opportunities for girls to participate in sports were still limited. Another Santa Fe graduate who attended and worked at the school during the late 1920s and early 1930s recalled, "I don't think there were any girls teams" (*First One Hundred Years*, March 31, 1987). A third person who graduated in 1937 and was interviewed by Hyer remembered, "'There was strict control because on Saturday afternoon the girls had to rest from after lunch until about four. It was just the idea that girls have to rest. So they did'"(Hyer 1990, 52).

Boarding school educators, however, had conflicting ideas about physical education for girls. One discussion, from Chilocco's *Indian School Journal* of February 1926, argued the case for girls' physical education in a particularly ironic fashion:

> Why physical education ... when all the background of Indian life pre-supposes for the race a heritage of sound health and an enviable physique? But ... could a really thoughtful person honestly believe, because a baby was sound at birth, and had traditionally healthy ancestors, that that one fact alone was guarantee for a sound body throughout the whole of life, even though the individual lived in ignorance of the laws of health which are as unyielding as all other laws of nature? In those by-gone days, to which distance now lends enchantment and romance, Indian men did endure untold hardship and exposure, and thrived on it; their women were sinuous and active, and some, at sixty and seventy, could walk long distances and run with ease. In those days, then, there was undoubtedly, foundation and ample justification for the simile, "as supple and straight as an Indian." But, and herein lies the crucial point, those people were healthy because they unwittingly practiced health rules, by living in the open, and by exercising, perforce, in their hunt for food, and in their flight for life itself in the face of the enemy.

This passage provides a vivid illustration of the contradictions involved in girls' physical education at boarding schools. It presents the same racial and cultural stereotypes of indigenous women used in earlier decades to justify their being sent to boarding school (physical strength, outdoor living, endurance). Yet it romanticizes these same activities, laments their passing, and argues for the necessity of boarding school physical education programs to fill in for what had been lost.

In spite of this call for girls' participation in sports, Chilocco still lacked adequate opportunities for girls during the 1930s. The annual report for 1936 states,

Not enough attention has been paid by the home department on play activities this year. More encouragement and direction of outdoor sports is needed; more spontaneous play and opportunities to mingle out in the open are likewise necessary. (*Annual Report for Chilocco Indian School* 1936)

Other school officials felt that athletic activities might, at the very least, keep girls busy and interested in their lives at boarding school. A 1931 letter from F. W. McDonald, director of athletics at Haskell, to the school's superintendent, for example, explicitly links the creation of a girls' intramural program with these issues:

Several years ago, when a spirit of unrest was prevalent among the girl students, I organized tournaments in various sports, in which the girls took a great deal of interest, and I am positive did much to afford them recreation and exercise. (McDonald 1931)

It is not clear what that "spirit of unrest" was. However, Child discovered that there was a rebellion at Haskell among students attending the school in October 1919. Five girls and four boys were expelled for taking part (Child 1993, 275). McDonald's letter reveals a level of negotiation involved in the implementation of athletic programs and in the way that students spent their leisure. What is more, it suggests that this negotiation was serious business, that schools had a great deal at stake in monitoring and controlling how students played, but that they also had to allow the students to play.

Boys were provided greater opportunity to participate in sports, but the orientation of their physical education was also deeply seated in the gender ideologies of boarding schools. As Barbara Ehrenreich and Deirdre English argue, within middle-class ideology of the early twentieth century, "experts" in psychology, family counseling, education, and medicine came to see sports as a primary means of teaching masculine values to boys in families, particularly as fathers came to be seen as largely absent from the day-to-day life of a home: "The world of sports became a sort of all-male subdrama within the larger family sex-role performance—

the only setting where fathers could pass on the ancient male values of competitiveness, male solidarity, and physical prowess" (Ehrenreich and English 1989, 247). Native American boys at boarding schools were often seen as the children of emasculated men incapable of adequately raising their sons in a modern world.

Discussion of boys' sports tended to emphasize their importance as a vehicle for teaching masculine values and character traits. The Haskell Institute course bulletin in 1940 expressed this theme, associating participation in athletics with moral character and masculinity, under a section describing the sports programs for boys at the school:

> Haskell provides a varied athletic program of intramural and interscholastic competition. This is done with a keen realization that clean sport affords students opportunity for personal development in health and character. Every phase of athletic activity is used as a means of guiding students to true manliness.... The program is sufficiently varied to assure every student an opportunity for participation in his favorite sport.... This activity will contribute to the development of his health, character, and personality in such a way as to further him to the road of successful living. (*Information Bulletin [Haskell]* 1940/41, 27)

Whereas for girls physical education tended to be dominated by exercises, for boys it tended to be dominated by athletic contests and sports. Chilocco's 1936 annual report provides a vivid example of this. Although boys did participate in marching, calisthenics, tumbling, pyramid building, dumbbell exercises, and other gymnastic drills, the report gives far more attention to intramural and interscholastic sports:

> This year every boy in school took part in intramural games. Every boy belonged to an organization and his organization was given points for wins, sportsmanship, number of participants and the attendance of the members of the organization that are not actual [*sic*] playing at the time. (*Annual Report for Chilocco Indian School* 1936)

Such intramural sports were not only important as recreation, but at Chilocco, they also served as farm teams for the varsity squads. The report's description of this system illustrates the degree to which intramural boys' sports were significant part of their social life:

> The boys who are outstanding in the intermural [*sic*] games of base ball, basketball, football and boxing are chosen to represent the school in the varsity games of the above named sports. When they join the varsity squad, they are no longer elgible [*sic*] for the intermural games in that particular sport. Sometimes it is pretty hard to get them to join the varsity squads because the rivalry within their groups is so great.

The gendered behavior that boarding schools advanced centered around self-control and discipline. Boarding schools were also concerned with the sexual behavior and desires of boys and did a great deal to monitor their lives in this regard. The *Annual Report for Chilocco Indian School* for 1934/35, for example, stated that boys were tested for venereal disease once a month. Schools expressed particular concern with the way that boys internalized the discipline that they learned in school, and as with female students, much of the schools' efforts centered upon attention to student leisure time. The 1935 narrative report by Harry S. Keller, the boys' adviser at Chilocco, expresses this effort:

> Our purpose as a department is character building. To develop character traits that embodies [*sic*] principles that will help the boy to be a better citizen. To live a wholesome life in the community in which he lives. Through proper grouping of the boys, and in cooperation with all employees organize and administer a home training program and supervision of the boys' free time, direct their interests into lives that will develop standards of value, purpose, ideals and proper attitudes. (*Annual Report for Chilocco Indian School* 1934/35)

For boys, the disciplinary lessons that they learned about leisure time were strongly linked to the vocational orientation of their boarding school education. From the founding of the boarding schools in the late nineteenth century, the curricula stressed vocational trades for boys. This remained true during the 1930s. Although the Collier administration at the BIA sought to reform education for Native Americans, education officials in the bureau still avoided the implementation of a curriculum that would prepare either female or male students for college. Historian Joe Sando, who attended the Santa Fe Indian School during the 1930s, remembers, in a documentary video, that

> [t]he policy of the bureau was that our parents did not have the financial standing to afford college for us. Consequently college was never promoted or we were never told that there was such a thing as a chance to go to college, so they taught us the trades because they figured that instead of becoming farmers when we went home, we would be able to use some of the things that we learned there back home, you know, as cabinet makers, carpenters, electricians, plumbers, and cement finishers. (Reyna et al. 1987)

In a 1935 letter to Chilocco's Superintendent Correll criticizing the school's emphasis on boxing, John Collier defined the mission of Indian boarding schools in a way that confirms Sando's observation:

> I believe in athletic training of all sorts for the students in our vocational schools, but you must keep in mind that their vocational education is the primary object of their attendance and that athletic contests with teams from various parts of the country are of secondary importance and must not be permitted to interfere with their vocational training. (Collier 1935)

The training of boys to be industrial workers focused as much on behavior during leisure time as it did on the learning of specific skills. Stanley Aronowitz, in his work on the education of working-class youth, argues that within capitalist structures of work, play, and leisure, play makes up a "second world of childhood" opposed to that of school, family, and work. In its vocational orientation, boarding schools taught male students to separate (and as a consequence, denigrate) work from other aspects of life, to forfeit control of work to a larger plan or authority. Drawing from the work of British historian E. P. Thompson, Aronowitz notes that working-class children understand, as Sando does, that social mobility after school is an illusion. For them, school is something to be endured. Aronowitz writes that "capitalism forces children to regard play and most adults to regard leisure as the core of their self-controlled lives. It is here alone that the chance remains to escape domination" (Aronowitz 1973, 60–82).

Although school administrators hoped that sports would provide a space in which leisure could be "productively" occupied, there is also evidence that those who attended boarding schools gained a great deal of pleasure from these events and made them their own. As one graduate of the Pipestone and Flandreau Indian Schools (located just a few miles from one another in southwestern Minnesota and eastern South Dakota) told me during a group interview with fellow former students on May 13, 1995, sporting events gave him the "chance to get out of that stupid school." Both males and females often reported that campus life was confining and that they grew weary of life within the walls of an Indian school. Some ran away, but few got far, and punishments for running away were among the most severe that one could get. Weekly entertainment events, such as those surrounding games, were important. They are often among former students' fondest memories of boarding school. Juanita Cata from San Juan Pueblo attended Santa Fe Indian School in the early 1940s and was interviewed in the late 1960s as part of the Doris Duke Oral History Project. When asked about the "good time" she had at boarding school, she remembered,

> We have dances on Saturday night, football game, basketball game, and we have movies like that and we have a big gym. And all we have to do is pay for tickets for $1.25, I guess it was at that time. And we buy tickets for the whole year around. And when we go we just show the tickets, it was nice at that time. (Cata 1968)

During the oral history interviews that I conducted, I found that student memories of sporting events on campus often were mixed with tales either of mischief or of circumvention of rules related to gender. For example, in the group interview I conducted on May 13, 1995, with Pipestone and Flandreau graduates, when I asked one man if he played sports, he replied, "I wasn't an athlete, I was a lover." This broke us all up in laughter. Later I asked the group, "Did girls have any sports when you were there?" He cut in, "Yeah, trying to keep away from the boys." Once again, everyone laughed, and the woman who had introduced me to the group yelled out, "Track!"

The same man later went on to discuss his socializing with girls as a deliberate flaunting of school rules:

> Well, like at Pipestone, they had, they'd have, they had their rules. But the, their rules didn't apply to them. They only applied to us. See, like one of our instructors, a male supervisor at the house, at the building, you know, well, you kids you can't be sneaking out with girls at night. What was he doing? He was sneaking the girls out . . . and I thought what the hell, you know? If he can't bide, abide by the rules, why should I? So I started doing it.
>
> [Another male, who had gone to Pipestone a few years after this man, chuckles.]
>
> He caught me [looking to the other man] . . . what? He caught me and threatened to beat the daylights out of me, and I told him, you go right ahead. I said, "I'll pass around what you've been doing. I know what you've been doing. Don't give me none of your B. S.," I told him. "You can beat the daylights out of me if you want, but I'll get back at you."

The man who laughed said he did not remember the supervisors and matrons behaving in this manner. However, others have reported sexual abuse by supervisors and teachers at boarding schools.[2] Such a story is particularly significant in light of the regulation, control, and surveillance placed upon student sexuality at boarding schools. It reveals not only how such rules confined the behavior of students but also the amount of power it gave those in supervisory positions. Although some during the group interviews remembered their matrons and boys' advisers as "nice," or even simply "strict," students were still extremely vulnerable to them while at boarding school. Many of the memories shared that day during the group interview revolved around the breaking of rules and around more general recollections of pranks and hijinks or of aggravating a particularly strict matron or supervisor. One remembered trying to sneak into town but getting caught and punished. Another recalled, "We used to sneak to town, but never get caught though." They talked of joyrides in cars, riding pigs in the barn, and running away. The man who claimed he was a "lover" disclosed, "I snuck off with a bunch of girls and snuck in a haystack. I was coming back home, and we asked this farmer if we could get something to eat. Sure, they fed us, then they put us in a truck and brought us back."

Recalling their days at Flandreau, they told me that sporting events were an important time for socializing on campus, and they implied that these events provided them with a momentary break from the kind of discipline and supervision revealed in school documents:

FEMALE GRADUATE: You know, you went out there, and if somebody else was in a different class, you'd say, okay, we'll meet here, and there, and first, second rung of the bleachers or wherever.

BLOOM: Right.

MALE 1: I mean they didn't separate them. They all, boys and girls sat together. I mean, they sat, they sat . . .

MALE 2: Along the football field.

MALE 1: They didn't separate them.

MALE 2: The football field was just a meeting place for the boys and girls.

[Laughter]

FEMALE: It was about the only place.

[Hearty laughter]

When females could participate in sports, they had a chance to behave in ways that they were not always allowed in other settings. A woman from Santa Clara Pueblo who graduated Santa Fe Indian School in 1929 recalled, "'I had lots of fun at the school because I was a basketball player and I looked forward to playing basketball. . . . I was better at playing basketball because I was mean and rough!" (quoted in Hyer 1990, 52).

Boarding school officials closely associated athletic and physical education programs with gender ideologies that they hoped to impart to students. School curricula openly discouraged females from playing competitive athletics, or even from engaging in strenuous physical activity. Instead, they promoted passivity, sexual restraint, and domestic femininity by emphasizing indoor activity and light exercise. However, both female and male students used sports and popular culture in ways that spoke to such curricular goals. For many students, having fun was important because it provided an escape from the regulation and discipline they experienced daily, particularly with regard to their sexuality. In oral history interviews, former students expressed a folk culture among students that often involved tricks, pranks, or stories about ways that students struggled with schools over rules guiding sexual behavior. Sports spectatorship offered some an opportunity to get away from the surveillance they experienced and to circumvent rules that were directed toward the management of their sexuality. For others, sports were a resource for expressing pleasure and enjoyment, emotions that are not often associated with life at Indian boarding schools and that school officials often seem to have found politically dangerous.

Richard Henry Pratt, founder of Carlisle Indian School and superintendent between 1879 and 1904. Pratt recognized the public relations possibilities for the school within such sports as football, but he also expressed ambivalence over the kind of image that successful athletic programs gave the school. Photograph courtesy of Cumberland County Historical Society, Carlisle, Pennsylvania.

Three baseball players at Carlisle Indian School in 1879 or 1880, just after the school opened. Left to right: Harry Kohpay (Osage), Robert Gem (unknown), and Paul Lovejoy (Omaha). Photograph courtesy of Cumberland County Historical Society, Carlisle, Pennsylvania.

Glenn S. "Pop" Warner, head football coach at Carlisle Indian School (1899–1904; 1907–1914), an early prototype of the hard-nosed coach driven to win. Photograph courtesy of Cumberland County Historical Society, Carlisle, Pennsylvania.

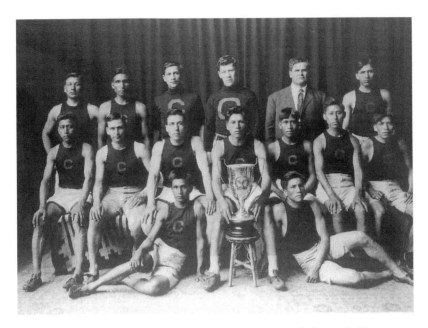

Warner stands with Carlisle Indian School's 1909 track team, which included Jim Thorpe (Sac and Fox; back row, third from right), who would win gold medals in the decathlon and pentathlon in the 1912 Olympics in Stockholm, and Louis Tewanima (Hopi; front row, extreme right), who won silver medals in the 5,000- and 10,000-meter races in the same Olympic games. Photograph courtesy of Cumberland County Historical Society, Carlisle, Pennsylvania.

The Carlisle Indian School football team at practice. Photograph courtesy of
Cumberland County Historical Society, Carlisle, Pennsylvania.

In 1926, the Haskell Institute celebrated its homecoming with the dedication of a new 10,000-seat stadium funded almost entirely from donations provided by Native Americans around the United States. This cover of the homecoming game's official program portrays the event as one that advanced the social progress of Native Americans. The stadium dedication and a powwow that accompanied it, however, raised concern among many in the Bureau of Indian Affairs and among missionaries, who worried that the forces advancing assimilation had lost control of Indian education. Courtesy of Kansas Collection, University of Kansas Libraries.

The football team of the Haskell Institute in Lawrence, Kansas, during the 1920s. Many called Haskell the "Carlisle of the West" because it also played and often beat the best collegiate football teams in the nation. Photograph courtesy of Kansas Collection, University of Kansas Libraries.

A baseball team from the Pipestone Indian School in southwestern Minnesota, probably in the early teens of the twentieth century. Photograph courtesy of Pipestone County Historical Society, Pipestone, Minnesota.

A girls' basketball team at the Haskell Institute posing in the early 1920s. Photograph courtesy of Kansas Collection, University of Kansas Libraries.

Girls were typically encouraged to participate in only limited forms of recreational play outdoors, such as the kind found in this photo of the "girls' playground" at the Pipestone Indian School. Photograph courtesy of Pipestone County Historical Society.

A group of female students at the Haskell Institute performs exercises during the 1920s. Physical educators at boarding schools regularly measured and weighed female students, and students had to perform physical exercises to "correct" body postures that educators saw as "improper." Photograph courtesy of Library of Congress, Washington, D.C.

Female students at the Santa Fe Indian School during the 1930s play softball. At that time boarding schools offered few opportunities for interscholastic female sports. Most girls who played sports had to do so on an intramural basis. Photograph courtesy of Gilbert Washburn Collection; reprinted by permission of Sally Hyer.

Girls at the Santa Fe Indian School participate in archery class. Photograph courtesy of Gilbert Washburn Collection; reprinted by permission of Sally Hyer.

Students from the Santa Fe Indian School perform in a track meet. Many students were able to translate Native American traditions of distance running into success on the track at boarding school. Photograph courtesy of Gilbert Washburn Collection; reprinted by permission of Sally Hyer.

Students from the Santa Fe Indian School perform in a track meet. Photograph courtesy of Gilbert Washburn Collection; reprinted by permission of Sally Hyer.

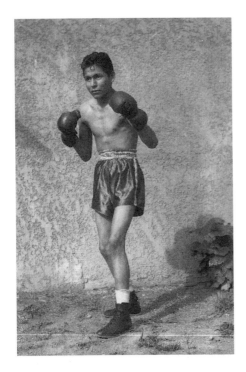

A boxer for the Santa Fe Indian School poses for the camera in the 1930s. Beginning in the early 1930s, many athletes found a spotlight in this new, controversial sport. Photograph courtesy of Gilbert Washburn Collection; reprinted by permission of Sally Hyer.

A boxer for the Santa Fe Indian School during the 1930s. Photograph courtesy of the Gilbert Washburn Collection; reprinted by permission of Sally Hyer.

The Pipestone Indian School gymnasium, where students would gather to meet friends and where many remembered seeing the Harlem Globetrotters play. Basketball games at the gym were occasions for students to meet and socialize outside of the boundaries of normal campus discipline. Photograph courtesy of Pipestone County Historical Society.

A bout fought at the Santa Fe Indian School during the late 1930s. Boxing was important in student popular culture, and many took pride in their school's fighters' accomplishments in bouts against other boarding schools and in amateur fights against nonnative opponents. Photograph courtesy of Gilbert Washburn Collection; reprinted by permission of Sally Hyer.

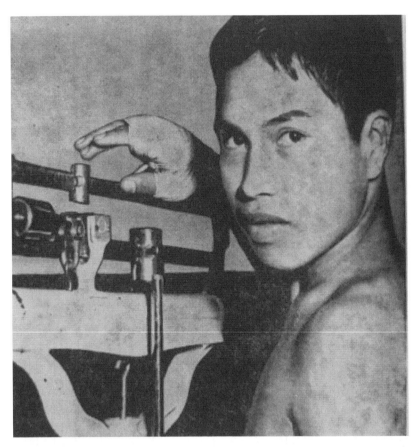

The caption below this photograph, printed in an edition of the *Indian Leader* from 1947, reads, "Making weight and staying physically fit is the secret of Boxing Success." In official publications, students often tied boxing to the virtues associated with hard work and discipline, which contrasted with the image of decadence and savagery that many in the Bureau of Indian Affairs linked to the sport. Photograph courtesy of Library of Congress, Washington, D.C.

# CHAPTER 5

# Narratives of Boarding School Life

Early on in my writing about sports at federally operated boarding schools for Native Americans, I decided to include oral history interviews with former students as a primary resource. The previous chapters have illustrated how boarding school students generated meanings from athletics, meanings that often differed from and even ran counter to the intentions of boarding school promoters, social reformers, and journalists. This is what I had hoped to learn by listening to the ways that former students remembered sports.

Even before I ever conducted an oral history interview, I had a sense that sports were an important part of the narratives that many Native Americans constructed of their boarding school lives. Published biographies and autobiographies (often presented as "told to" an anthropologist who collected the narrative) often contain passages in which the author recounts experiences at boarding school and memories of athletics at these institutions. Asa "Ace" Daklugie, the son of the Apache leader and warrior Juh and the nephew of Geronimo, remembered sports as a particularly significant aspect of his life at Carlisle. In his autobiography (told to researcher Eve Ball), he says, "The thing that pulled me through was the athletic training at Carlisle" (Ball 1980, 146). Narcissus Duffy Gayton, a descendant of Apaches who were sent to Carlisle along with Daklugie, was sent by her parents to Albuquerque Indian School during the 1930s and early 1940s. Her biographer, Ruth McDonald Boyer, writes that Gayton "dreaded" regular Saturday night dances and that she "preferred to watch basketball, football, and baseball games where there was keen competition with the athletes of other schools in the vicinity." Gayton herself "developed considerable skill in tennis, playing with Mescalero, and Elsie Beyal, a Navajo" (Boyer and Gayton 1992, 303). Hopi Don Talayesva, in his autobiography titled *Sun Chief*, remembers life at Sherman Institute in Riverside, California. He tells a story of extreme alienation, loneliness, and illness that brought him near to death, but he also remembers, "I . . . played baseball some and enjoyed it very much" (Talayesva 1942, 131). John Fire/Lame Deer recalled that boarding school was a cold, inhuman place of discipline and drudgery, but he also writes, "I was a good athlete. I busted a kitchen window once playing stickball. After that I never hit so good again." He concludes, "I think in the end I got the better of that school. I was more of an Indian when I left than when I went in. My back had been tougher than the many straps they had worn out on it" (Fire/Lame Deer and Erdoes 1972, 35–36).

All of these narrators remember sports in a positive light, even if they had negative memories of boarding school in general. Sports certainly do not play a prominent role in Native Americans' overall narratives. Nevertheless, almost all published recollections of boarding school by Native Americans contain some mention of athletics. Of course, this might be more a reflection of a discourse common to those who edit these books. I may have simply run across a narrative structure or formula that is familiar and comfortable to the anthropologists or oral historians who often compile such autobiographies. Yet if all of these narrators mentioned sports when they discussed their memories of boarding school, this might just as easily be evidence that memories of athletics occupy a widely recognized critical space in narratives of boarding school life for Native Americans.

At the same time that I was eager to conduct oral histories, however, I was also somewhat apprehensive. I am a non-Native, white scholar, and in order to conduct interviews, I traveled to communities and reservations far from my own home. What use would those I interviewed have for my work, and how would they receive me? Knowing the long history of academic and commercial exploitation of Native American language, religion, and culture, not to mention the history of boarding schools themselves, or even 500 years of Euro-American conquest, occupation, and ethnic cleansing, I could not blame anyone who might greet me with something less than as their unqualified confidence. I would have to work hard at establishing my research as an equal exchange rather than as a practice in intellectual extraction.

Such concerns are not just my own. They have been a core part of the criticism that many Native American writers and scholars have directed toward academics for decades. Vine Deloria Jr. articulated them in his 1969 manifesto *Custer Died for Your Sins*, in which he provided a stinging attack of anthropological studies. In a famous chapter of that book, he mocks scholars who search for an "authentic" Native American "folk," writing that they are only engaged in an activity that justifies their own professional position and that they do little for the people that they "study" (Deloria Jr. 1969, 78–100). Contemporary works in anthropology and history by James Clifford, Michael M. J. Fischer, George E. Marcus, Devon A. Mihesuah, and Renato Rosaldo have responded to the kind of critique fashioned by Deloria and have called for collaborative approaches to fieldwork, approaches that respect the critical insights and voices of the person being interviewed and of the narrative that the interviewee constructs.[1]

Understanding how sports help to shape a narrative might bring about the kinds of critical insights that these scholars discuss, particularly given how often sports arise in published autobiographical accounts. Early in my interviews, however, I had a somewhat comic exchange that suggested it was not going to be easy to get beyond traditional fieldwork relationships. One of the Navajo men who had boxed for Santa Fe Indian School began our interview before I asked any questions by recounting the roots of Navajo language and history within a larger Athabascan heritage. He did so in such a routinized fashion that it almost seemed as if he felt he knew what I wanted to hear and was just going to get it out of the way as quickly as possible. After we talked for a short while, I asked him some questions about boarding school sports. This topic was so far from what he seemed to expect to talk about that he furrowed his brow and tried to get straight what it was I wanted to know: "Indian ways by participating in sports, or what is it?" Once he got into talking about his recollections of his boarding school life and of sports, however, he relaxed and moved into more of a storytelling mode. His boxing career was clearly something that he remembered vividly, even if he did not expect someone like me to take any particular interest in it.

People were not usually quite so surprised by my interests, and they eagerly told their stories of sports and boarding school life. For example, the group interview that I conducted on the Fond du Lac Anishinabe (Ojibwa) reservation near Duluth, Minnesota, was actually set up without my knowledge by a woman I had contacted. I had originally intended to interview just her. But before I flew out to Minnesota to meet her, she told me that she had taken out an advertisement in a local paper for people to participate and that people were getting excited. When I arrived at her house, she invited me in for coffee, introduced me to her husband, and told me that she had reserved a conference room for the group interview in the new Fond du Lac Community College that had been built on the reservation. She and her husband took me on a tour of the reservation, including the new Head Start day care center where she worked, and then took me out for lunch at the new casino. She told me that its proceeds helped to pay for much of the new construction on the reservation, but she also said that she thought the place was fun and liked to take her vacations gambling at reservation casinos. She brought her own tape player to record the interview, and when it was all done she gave me a pile of gifts—a small dream catcher for my son, a bag of wild rice harvested on the reservation, and a large dream catcher for me and my wife. About this last gift, she said that she remembered that I had told her of a miscarriage my wife had had in the fall, and she advised me to put it behind our bed, for as she put it, "You know."[2]

Although I was not often greeted with such extraordinary warmth, those whom I interviewed were often eager to tell me about their experiences with sports and at boarding school. One of the two Navajo men I interviewed who had boxed for Santa Fe Indian School had become a well-known artist, but he expressed his appreciation to me that I had taken an interest in his less-well-known athletic career. After we completed our interview, he asked if I could get any old photographs of Santa Fe Indian School athletes, and if I could send him any other materials that might still exist from his days at Santa Fe.

Relatives of those whom I interviewed but who have since died have also responded to the articles and transcripts that I sent. For some, the memories of sports that were discussed during interviews were not something they had heard much about before. Others knew that sports and boarding school had been an important part of the life experienced by the person I interviewed and were happy to have these memories recorded.

Most others who record oral history report similar experiences with the people whom they interview and who narrate stories to them. There are undoubtedly many reasons for this, but in chronicling oral history the interviewer is always faced with vast, diverse experiences that resist most broad generalizations about the past. As George Lipsitz writes, though people need to understand the past in order to locate the relationship of their individual lives within larger collective experiences, "the complexities and pluralities of the past always resist definitive evaluation and summary" (Lipsitz 1990, 21). Outside of occasional references to Jim Thorpe, most written narratives of Native American history have not treated sports (and have only very recently begun to treat boarding schools) as something of particular importance. I think this is reflected in the narratives I heard from former boarding school students. In both the surprise expressed that anyone would be interested in this history and in the eager responses to my curiosity about Native American sports, I learned that stories about athletics are not widely known or circulated outside of Native American communities. The invisibility of an aspect of twentieth-century life that was so important to many Native Americans illustrates how difficult it is to write about and draw conclusions about the past; it illustrates that history is, in the words of Lipsitz, "precious and incommunicable."

The neglect of Native American sports also reflects a tendency among academics not to treat sports as a particularly significant or complex cultural phenomenon. Michael Novak called attention to this intellectual snobbery in the mid-1970s in his book *The Joy of Sports*. Unfortunately, Novak sometimes assumes an angry, defensive stance in his writing about sports, and he overcompensates for their denigration by arguing that they have become "religion." In doing so, he isolates sports from social experience and ultimately only further exacerbates the problem. Such analysis might provide for pleasurable reading by sports fans, but it oversimplifies the place of sports in the contemporary world and further encourages understandings of athletics as relatively uncomplicated and unconnected to social and historical realities (Novak 1976).

Rather than addressing the lack of intellectual attention payed to sports by countering, as Novak does, that "history is an escape," I would argue that the importance of sports, as with any cultural form or social institution, lies in its location within historical contexts and dialogues. Lipsitz has argued persuasively on the importance of analyzing popular music this way. Drawing upon the theories of Russian literary critic Mikhail Bakhtin, Lipsitz asks us to understand rock and roll as part of a complex historical conversation "embedded in collective history and nurtured by the ingenuity of artists interested in fashioning icons of opposition" (Lipsitz 1990, 99). Lipsitz argues that popular music is "polysemic"—or "filled with contradictory voices representing the contradictions of social life" (100).

Sports do not have authors in the same way that popular music (even with its collectively authored character) does, so it is harder to see within the practice of sports "artists interested in fashioning icons of opposition." However, this does not mean that we cannot understand sports as a polysemic cultural form that emerges out of, engages, and is meaningful within the context of complex historical dialogues "representing the contradictions of social life." Even among whites, most sports historians agree that athletics in the late nineteenth and early twentieth centuries emerged representing discourses of white, elite, Anglo-Protestant masculine virility, sacrifice, and virtue on the one hand, but also that it emerged providing a means for expression of hedonistic consumer desire, fun, and working-class ethnic rivalry on the other. The varied reactions and policies of white leaders toward sports at boarding schools for Native Americans reflect this ambivalence and, in turn, the contradictory historical dialogues that have surrounded athletics more generally in the United States.

In addition, like any other cultural phenomenon, sports are never experienced in isolation. They often involve or are interwoven with other popular culture texts and social institutions. From the beginning of the twentieth century, sports leagues had been firmly established as extensions of schools, businesses, community organizations, and ethnic enclaves. They were extensively covered by news media outlets and exploited by advertisers, and they were experienced in the electronic media of radio and television right alongside jazz, blues, rock and roll, soap operas, variety shows, and news programs. Each popular culture form contains its own historical dialogues, which were thus juxtaposed against and understood in relation to those presented through sports.

For Native Americans, as with other minority groups in the twentieth century, sports have had an especially polysemic character. Recalling Native American sports history evokes a variety of historical voices in dialogue over issues of conquest, survival, assimilation, negotiation, and resistance. In a recent article, Philip Deloria explores this in a discussion of the athletic career of his grandfather, Vine Deloria Sr., an Episcopalian minister and Lakota elder. Deloria recalls that his grandfather, while sick with Alzheimer's disease, would recall his heroics as a football star at St. Stephen's (Bard) College as a young man. Deloria writes, "The more I thought about this exchange, the more compelling it became. At some primal level, my grandfather seemed to define himself neither as a Christian minister nor as a Lakota elder, but as an athlete" (Deloria 1996, 323).

Rather than concluding, however, that these athletic memories were only trivial bits of memory that survived his grandfather's dementia, Deloria recognizes that sports were something more important and complex. Deloria argues that they were an important part of how Native Americans, particularly at the turn of the century, negotiated their identities and social positions within the circumstances they faced. "For my grandfather," writes Deloria, "race, religion, culture, and family were inextricably tangled with his feats on the playing field" (323). Deloria notes that his father, the famous Lakota lawyer and author Vine Deloria Jr., remembered harsh government agents and missionaries coming to reservations. But even as their work sought to annihilate indigenous cultures and identities, it also provided some opportunities for alternative practices. Sports were one important avenue that appealed to his grandfather, as well as to many others. Native Americans had their own sporting practices long before contact with Europeans, and they "welcomed the introduction (often by missionaries) of American-style football, baseball, and basketball, easily enfolding these newcomers into extant cultural traditions." As much as such sports often provided an avenue for the expression of a "refigured warrior tradition," however, they also "provided an entree into American society—a chance to beat Whites at their own games, an opportunity to get an education, and, even at its most serious, an occasion for fun and sociality" (326).

Deloria recognizes that historians must be careful not to engage in "uncritical celebration" of such cultural practices and need to always be careful to understand such expressions within the context of unequal power relations and oppression. Yet it is also important to understand how, within such contexts, Native Americans have been able to draw upon the tools of dominant society and use them for their own purposes:

> It is customary to sum up [federal and missionary] policies in terms of assimilation, resistance, and conflict: Did White Americans erase native culture? Did Indianness survive? Any change, of course, tends to be coded as declension—in this case, as the incremental death of "traditional" native culture. Alternatively, one can celebrate the vitality of "culture" itself as a meta-concept, pointing to the inevitability and legitimacy of its continual refigurings.... Again and again, [Native Americans] created new Indian worlds, fusing diverse cultures or fitting themselves into the interstices between a core native "tradition" and new practices introduced from the American periphery. (323–25)

One can appreciate the dialogic character of Native American sports history by listening, as Philip Deloria did, to the memories of those who played sports at boarding schools and on reservations. Oral history narratives conducted with former boarding school students not only recount the details of past heroics or even of particular teams and athletes. They connect boarding school experiences to narratives and histories circulated through popular culture and leisure.

What was probably the most compelling story I found in this regard did not come from a published source or from an oral history interview that I conducted. Rather, it is from an interview I found collected among oral history transcripts at the Arizona State Museum in Tucson as part of a collection funded by the Doris Duke Foundation.[3] As with published autobiographies of Native Americans, sports actually appear in only a small portion of the interview that Elizabeth Euler and Patricia McGee conducted in 1967 with Arthur Harris, a member of the Yavapai tribe near Prescott, Arizona. Yet sport, leisure, and play occupy a critical position in his story. Harris remembers particular sporting events and leisure activities in ways that can be read as helping to shape his boarding school memories as a counternarrative, one that critically reflects upon race, national identity, and assimilation. I have edited the interview to include the core aspects of Harris's story, upon which I will be commenting. However, I have also included some of the questions asked by Euler and McGee to provide a sense of the contexts in which these answers were produced:[4]

> HARRIS: When I was a child, about six or seven, I remember ... that the government awfully forceful to give the Indians, young Indians, an education. There was a, a boarding school there, and I remember, us youngsters used to would go up on the hills and, and make a, a rock wall in a, in a cave, we'd hide there so the, the, the policeman, the Indian policeman wouldn't see us to take us to the school. We used to hide there quite a bit, but later on some were caught and they put 'em in school. . . . But I was not caught, I was the only child at the time.

EULER: You were your parents' only child?

HARRIS: At that time . . .

EULER: Did your parents help you hide? They try to hide you, or you. . . ?

HARRIS: No, I, I hide myself . . . With the other children. They'd get, come early, you know, we'd carry a little lunch with us to stay up there all day because the, the policeman hunted us all the time, but I finally, after seeing the Indian children wearing nice clothes and good shoes, and I thought to myself, just like I told you, my hair was way down to here.

EULER: Down below your waist, huh?

HARRIS: Yeah, and I guess I was pretty dirty. At any rate, I wanted to become educated. My father and mother didn't want me to go to school. They wanted me to stay there help my mom farm, we had a little farm, we raised a lot of things . . . corn, watermelon, squash, the likes of that. . . . So they, they didn't want me to go school, but I ran away from my parents, then I went to school.

EULER: There at San Carlos [a reservation boarding school].

HARRIS: Yeah. I was sitting up on a hill there. I remember the Apache boy come to me. He says, I remember the words very well, "Do you want to go to school?" I got up and walked. We went to the school. They gave me good clothes. . . . They, my parents couldn't do nothing with me there after, after I got in school . . .

EULER: How old were you?

HARRIS: More likely nine, ah, ten.

EULER: Did they, ah, make you, ah, change anything about yourself? Like your hair, or. . . ?

HARRIS: Yeah, they caught, ah, they cut my hair off, and they give me good clipping so a new crop would come up. I remember that very well, and give me a place, give me underclothes, nice clothes to wear. I took a bath in tub, they didn't have no showers them days so I had a tub bath . . .

EULER: Did you want these things?

HARRIS: Yes, I want it very much to be like the, the boys that have plain clothes. . .

MCGEE: What kind of clothes did you have before you started to school?

HARRIS: I just had a waist, hang down to above my knee . . . Just a, ah, flour sack. . . . Mama opened the side of the . . . my arms were bare, ah, made a hole up where the sewed part is, that was for my neck to go through ... I mean my head to go through. That's what I had to wear.

EULER: Did you have shoes?

HARRIS: No shoes at all, my calluses were that thick ...

MCGEE: And they did not give the children clothes until they went to school?

HARRIS: Yes, most all of them.

In the interview, Harris goes on to say that he was not allowed to speak Yavapai at boarding school. The school forced students to only speak English. All the same, at one point a group of linguistic researchers from the University of Michigan came to visit, and they asked Harris to speak only in Yavapai, and not in English: "They even ask me, 'Do you sing an Indian song?' I sing two or three of them, and they, they got a kick out of it. One of them got up and danced back and forth, and you know, I, I was tickled."

After Harris had been at San Carlos a year, the superintendent of the school asked him to transfer to Phoenix Indian School. He spent eight years there and graduated in 1910. He told the researchers the following story:

HARRIS: When I graduated there, before I graduated there, my teacher told us about Booker T. Washington, his, his write-up about *Up from Slavery*, remember that book?

EULER: I've read it.

HARRIS: Well, she says, "A Negro wanted to get, ah, an education. He went to Hampton, Virginia. He cleans school rooms, three or four times, sweep it." He tells it in the *Up from Slavery* that he, his teacher was pretty strict Yankee, Yankee ... woman.... She was pretty strict. So Booker T. Washington worked there and got his education. He worked hard. So the teacher read us the story. Said to myself, "If the Negro can do that, I can do it. So I make up my mind when I graduated in 1910, May the 13th. My principal speaker was Governor Sloan.... My ... the Indians that graduated with me were pretty bright, they're pretty smart people. I'm not.

EULER: Well, you seem to be coming along [chuckle].

HARRIS: [Chuckle] Anyway, I says to myself, "If that Negro can do it, I can do it." So I make my mind up to go to Hampton. At that time, the government appropriated enough money for some Indian students to go to Hampton. So, in the, so in the summer of 1910, I played baseball up this, up, ah, Flagstaff. There was ah, a Yavapai woman that was a teacher at Hampton, ah, teach at Phoenix Indian School, Irene Tapashetto was her name, she'd been to Hampton. I found out that she had been to Hampton. There was two of them, Emma Burro was the other one. They're pretty smart women.

EULER: Both Yavapais.

HARRIS: Uh huh. So we got information from these two, it was a good school. They say that was the best school the Indian could get education, from Hampton Institute.[5] "Okay, I'm going to Hampton," so I made up my mind. I come to Prescott after leaving Flagstaff in 1910, right here.

EULER: Oh, did you go to play baseball in Flagstaff?

HARRIS: Yes.

EULER: For the Indian School, or for some other . . .

HARRIS: For the Indian School. . . . But, ah, they were professional ball players. We were not classified, but we just give 'em an exhibition of, of ball game. We picked, ah, on a Fourth of July, at that time Jack Johnson was fighting Jim Jeffers[6] over there in Reno. I heard all the fight story, I was at Flagstaff.

EULER: What team did you play against?

HARRIS: We played against Fort Wingate [another federally operated off-reservation boarding school for Native Americans] from New Mexico. . . . We beat 'em four to nothing. Next day, we played Flagstaff, but these Indians that represented the Indian school knew Morris, the catcher, William, Ernie Williams is the pitcher, we played against them before, and they're good ball players. We got beat pretty bad. I was the pitcher and the captain of the team. At any rate, we got beat on the fifth of July. . . . They treated us royal, everybody, a lot of the white people bet on the Indian team, and we got beat pretty bad, twelve to two.

Harris went on to explain that he went to work on the Santa Fe Railroad to earn money and go east to Hampton. He then responded to a question about whether he had gone to Carlisle to school:

You asked me whether I attended school at Carlisle or not, and I said, "No," but I went there in 1912, I saw Carlisle. I went there to, to see, see how the school was, I didn't intend to go to school there because, ah, the schooling there did not compare evenly with Hampton, see? Ours at Hampton was higher. I was there when Mr. Friedman and Mrs. Friedman were there. Mr. Friedman was the superintendent at Carlisle, and I met a student there named Marcus Carvahal, he's a Mexican, but he passed for Indian, and he went to school there. He, he saw me there, and we went to see Mr. Friedman and Mrs. Friedman, he was the superintendent.

Although he enjoyed his time at Hampton, Harris explained that the school lost its appropriation in 1912 from the federal government, so he had to work his way through. "Some Indian senator came there, saw the Indians mixed with the Negroes, he was afraid that they was going to intermarry with the Negroes so he, so he went back to, to Washington, he abolished the appropriation."

I had to pay my way through. I worked. I, I cleaned the rooms, then what little I make in the shop helped me out, but there was, there was enough money there that if you lacked a little bit why they, they got that money, ah, the, the government appropriated years back, they had enough there to help the Indians that cannot help themselves.

Harris also spent the summers working on farms in New England. One year, upon returning to the school, he was asked to sing in the school's traveling chorus. "The lady says, 'We want you to represent the Indians.' The Negroes have a chorus and a quartet. They travel all over the big, big summer resorts. They raise money for the school":

EULER: Were they singing? Singing?
HARRIS: Yes. Spiritual Songs. . . . And, ah, the lady says to me, "I want you to go with the singers, the chorus or the quartet. I want you to tell, tell about the Indians." I had to memorize that. Two or three different speeches because some places where we meet, we have to meet two or three times

at one, one place, so I have to, I can't tell the same story, I have to make another talk, you know ...

EULER: What did you say?

HARRIS: Well, I told the history of, ah, of my people, the Yavapai Indians first.... Then I, then I tell about how, how I went to school. Then what I was aiming for is to get a good education, to live among white people, and I have been. Well, we went on our tour. Some places the big money people give us a check for a thousand dollars, five hundred dollars, fifty dollars, whatever they want to donate to the school. They always mention Booker T. Washington, where Booker T. Washington went to school. Lot of the white people take to their singing, and I make a talk on the behalf of the Indians, practically all the Indians at times, but mostly on the history of my, myself ...

EULER: You were the only Indian.

HARRIS: Only Indian. Sometime I put on Indian paraphernalia, you know, look like an Indian.

EULER: What would you put on?

HARRIS: I would put on a, a belt here, a blouse here, a waist that hangs over like the Indians wear, you know. This lady ga ... gave me all those, then I put on a war bonnet, sometimes I, I pretend I know how to dance.

Harris tells a fascinating narrative, one that cannot be easily summarized or contained. I am most interested, however, in the complex and multiple dimensions of history that are woven throughout his story and in the significance of sports, and of popular culture more generally, to that narrative. When I first read this transcript, I was very confused. On the one hand, it conveys a story of brutality, of tribal police literally kidnapping children, taking them away from their families, and placing them in boarding schools where they would be forcefully assimilated and forced to speak only English.[7] Yet Harris also reports that he wanted to go to boarding school to escape the poverty of his reservation and his family.[8] He goes on to list as one of his heroes Booker T. Washington, a man who, for many, has served as a model of safe, subservient, African American assimilation. He reports how kindly white people treated his Phoenix

Indian School baseball team as they played the national pastime on a patriotic holiday, July 4, 1910. He almost models his own personal narrative after Washington's, to the extent that he even scrubbed the same floors at Hampton Institute that he read about Booker T. Washington scrubbing in *Up from Slavery* so that he could stay in school. And in recalling his time at Hampton, he tells of his travels around the country performing "Indianness"—just as the Hampton Choir performed "blackness" in a way that spoke for and was meant to represent "the race"—through dances that never existed within his tribal culture but that sound much more like those circulated and sold to whites within commercial film, pulp fiction, and wild west shows of the era.

All of this makes it sound as if Harris's story is a rather straightforward celebration of ideologies that have been a core aspect of dominant culture in the United States: ideologies such as those elevating individual success and upward mobility, nonwhite subservience, and white privilege and paternal responsibility. I have since discovered that this interview is not as straightforward as I initially thought it was. Instead, I have come to recognize what cultural historians and literary critics have termed "hidden transcripts" within the narrative that Harris creates. "Hidden transcripts" are "'daily conversations, folklore, jokes, songs, and other cultural practices' that challenge those in power and often arise in disguised form on stage" (Caponi-Tabery 1999), in public spaces controlled by the powerful. Gena Dagel Caponi-Tabery argues that such "hidden transcripts" were a core aspect of African American jump style in sports and popular culture—namely in basketball and in "jump" music of the 1940s and 1950s (Caponi-Tabery 1999).[9] These hidden transcripts are important not only for what they might say about Harris but for the clues they provide into the complex nature of boarding schools, Native American history, and the role of sports within these. Harris's story is particularly important for the way that it positions hidden transcripts relevant to a particular Native American history in dialogue with some that emerged from African American culture and history. Although sports are only a small portion of the part of Harris's narrative that I have presented, they are a crucially important aspect, for they are in dialogue with events and stories from the past that reflect critically upon the present. Harris's story might seem to accommodate those in power, but it is also about using dominant society to survive and about drawing upon hidden stories to fashion critique.

Harris's recollections of hiding from tribal police who were rounding up children to go to boarding school are among the most striking and disturbing in his narrative. Perhaps this makes it somewhat difficult to accept that he left the reservation as voluntarily as he presents it. Yet it is also important to place his recollections within the context of Yavapai history. In doing so, we might understand his narrative, and his presentation of memory, as one of active negotiation rather than of submission and defeat.

According to historian Stephen Trimble, the Yavapai people lived and roamed an area of more than 10,000,000 acres of what is now Arizona with relative freedom until the 1850s. They were made up of four general subtribes: Tolkapaya (Western Yavapai), Yavepe (Central Yavapai), Keweukapaya (Southeastern Yavapai), and the Wipukpaya (Northeastern Yavapai). They lived nomadically, traveling in bands of up to ten families. In winter they would gather in huts or caves in groups of up to a hundred families, and throughout the year they lived primarily by means of hunting and gathering (Trimble 1993, 231).

In 1863 white prospectors discovered gold in the Hassayampa River near what is now Prescott, Arizona. This attracted settlers, who soon came into conflict with the Yavapai who lived in that area. By 1865 the first farmers had begun to arrive and settle in the Verde Valley and other areas. In doing so they severely disrupted food-gathering grounds. Faced with starvation, Yavapai bands began to raid settlers in the region. The U.S. Army responded by sending troops to protect the settlers. In 1866 about 2,000 Yavapais decided to take up farming on the new Colorado River reservation that had been set up for them, but they were forced off this land and into the mountains after their farming settlements provoked competition with whites and with Mojave Indians. Trimble quotes the chairman of Camp Verde reservation, Ted Smith, as calling the period that ensued "a ten year Vietnam War" (1993, 233).

In 1871 General George Crook arrived to take command of the

army and to bring Yavapai and Apache raids on settlers to an end. He advocated the containment of Indians on reservations as well as their assimilation, and he set up the Rio Verde reservation in the Verde Valley. The Yavapais still had difficulty subsisting, and the raids continued. Calling the Yavapais "Apaches," a tribe that whites in the area had already demonized, Crook started an assault against the raiding tribes. In April 1873 Yavapai leader Chalipun surrendered to Crook, and in their captivity and starvation, many Yavapais began to die from disease. By the summer, the Rio Verde reservation's population had declined by one-third. In December 1873, the army massacred an entire Yavapai band (including babies and children) in what has become known as Skeleton Cave above the Salt River Canyon (Trimble 1993, 233–34).

Even after this devastation, many Yavapai were able to farm successfully on the Rio Verde reservation. Between 1874 and 1875, however, their success had begun to disturb government contractors, who found that the prosperity of the Yavapais had lessened their dependence upon rations. The contractors lobbied for the abolition of the Rio Verde reservation. In February 1875, they succeeded, and the Yavapai residents of the reservation were forced to march 150 roadless miles over mountains to the San Carlos Apache reservation, where they were relocated. At San Carlos, the Yavapais generally lived peacefully with the Apaches, but they were also an ethnic minority. They settled in a portion of the reservation, and there, like Harris's parents, many once more took up farming. By the 1880s, however, their irrigation system had been washed away in a series of floods, and by the 1890s, coal miners began to take an interest in their farming lands on San Carlos. Because of these pressures, the federal government reestablished the Rio Verde reservation. By 1901 most Yavapai had left San Carlos and returned to the Prescott area, Arlington, or Ft. McDonell (Trimble 1993, 234–37). Of the 1,500 who began the original walk to San Carlos in 1875, only 200 were alive in the 1890s when the Yavapai returned (Hinton and Watahomigie 1984, 165).

As a Yavapai living on San Carlos, Harris was a direct descendant of the people who had been removed there. His narrative places him as a child of those who had taken up farming in the region and who, after two decades of displacement, war, massacre, and forced relocation, were struggling to survive from day to day on a reservation that many did not consider to be their home. Harris's choice to leave for boarding school, then, must not be understood as a move from an "authentic," unmediated, indigenous social order into dominant society. It is far more accurate to understand it as one of many difficult choices facing Yavapais during that time period. It is particularly important that Harris represents his departure for boarding school as a choice, for in doing so, he becomes an actor in his own story, somebody who operates within the historically constructed choices made available to him.

In this same manner, Harris's decision to attend Hampton Institute seems on the surface to be an endorsement of assimilation. Yet the narrative that he tells about that time of his life actually evokes critical contradictions surrounding race and identity. One can see this by paying careful attention to the ways that sports and popular culture figure in Harris's narrative.

The Hampton Normal and Agricultural Institute in Hampton, Virginia, was originally created in 1868 to educate freed slaves. Samuel Chapman Armstrong, a former U.S. Army officer who had led an all-black troop during the Civil War, founded and ran the school, and it quickly built a strong reputation among reformers. Booker T. Washington was perhaps its best-known alumnus, and in his autobiographies and papers he wrote extensively of his experiences as a student at the school. In 1878 Armstrong decided to open Hampton's doors to a group of more than seventy Native American men, most of whom the U.S. Army had taken prisoner and held at Ft. Marion in St. Augustine, Florida, during the Red River War on the southern plains. Captain Richard Henry Pratt had been in charge of guarding these new students in Florida. Although he left Hampton only a year later to found Carlisle, Hampton Institute continued to serve as a boarding school for Native Americans, alongside its more established and numerous African American students, until 1923.[10]

Harris recalls that he learned of Hampton while a student at the Phoenix Indian School when a teacher had him read Booker T. Washington's memoir *Up from Slavery*. However, he made the decision to attend the school over the Fourth of July weekend in 1910 while participating in a baseball tournament playing for the Phoenix Indian School against both Indian and white teams. Even more significantly, he takes special care to remind his interviewers that July 4, 1910, was an eventful day in sports history. On that date, Jack Johnson, the first African American heavyweight boxing champion, successfully defended his title against a white fighter named Jim Jeffries in Reno, Nevada. He makes only a brief reference to this, but it shapes his narrative in very important ways.

The Johnson-Jeffries bout was one of the most publicized sporting events of its time. Newspaper coverage structured the drama surrounding the fight almost entirely around racial combat. Barred from fighting for the heavyweight title in the United States because of his race, Johnson had won it in Australia and returned home a champion. As such, he was finally able to schedule a title fight in the United States. Jeffries, an undefeated, retired white former champion, was his opponent.

Harris only says about the fight that his Phoenix Indian School team played an exhibition over the holiday against a white professional team and that "at that time Jack Johnson was fighting Jim Jeffers [*sic*] over there in Reno. I heard all the fight story, I was at Flagstaff." Yet the fight "story" intertwined with powerful discursive threads surrounding race and power. Media coverage around the United States framed the fight in terms of racial combat, mocking Johnson as, among other things, morally corrupt, intellectually deficient, arrogant, lazy, comically inept, and greedy. The *Chicago Daily Tribune*, for example, ran a daily comic strip, sometimes on its front page, called "Sambo Remo Rastus Brown— He Meets Jack in Reno Town," in which a minstrel comic character, after whom the comic gets its name, travels to the fight to meet Jack Johnson. The same paper ran special features penned by "Gentleman" Jim Corbett, who, the headline for the July 1, 1910, paper screamed, "says Black's Fear of White in Old Times Will Count on July 4." On the eve of the fight, the *Tribune* celebrated Jeffries as a "Son of Preacher" and vilified Johnson as a "Coward in Youth" who "Disliking Work, ... Takes up Fighting to Get Money." On July 5, the *Washington Post*, in an article "Race Clashes in Many Cities," and other newspapers reported that

Johnson had won the fight and that in the wake of his victory, race riots had erupted in New York (where whites set fire to a tenement occupied by African Americans), Ft. Worth, Roanoke, Atlanta, Kansas City, and several other cities and towns throughout the United States.

Given these circumstances, the Fourth of July weekend, 1910, would seem, at the very least, an inopportune time for a Native American to decide to attend a boarding school made famous as an educational institution for African Americans. This is particularly true in light of the fact that Harris's account of his own relationship with whites that weekend was positive. He reports that after his team lost to the professional team from Flagstaff, the town's white residents "treated us royal." He even goes so far as to state that many bet on his team, even though the Phoenix players lost badly to the professionals.

He does not explicitly discuss the contrast between the treatment he received and the reaction of whites to Jack Johnson's victory, but his mention of the event frames his decision to attend Hampton in an ironic fashion. The irony of his narrative rests upon race and racial discourses. He chooses a day marked by brutality and oppression directed against African Americans, during an era more largely defined by the imposition of a Jim Crow social order, by mob violence against African Americans, by the resurgence of the Ku Klux Klan, and by lynchings, to stake his own future in the Hampton Institute.

Of course, one might interpret this narrative as not being the least bit ironic. The hero who inspired Harris to attend Hampton, Booker T. Washington, was, after all, quite popular among a great many white leaders as a model of assimilation and accommodation. Unlike Jack Johnson, many whites felt that Washington was someone who "knew his place," and his own writings suggest that Washington saw Hampton as a school where Indians would learn theirs. After graduating from Hampton, Washington had returned to the school in 1880 to work as a supervisor for the newly arrived Native American students. He wrote extensively of his thoughts about Native Americans in the *Southern Workman*, a regularly printed publication of the Hampton Institute. His writings are every bit as condescending as anything that white reformers like Pratt wrote during that time, often portraying his students as childlike and primitive and expressing frustration with his Indian students who continued to wear clothes improperly, to observe habits that he felt were unhealthy, and to display difficulty adapting to "civilization" (Harlan et al. 1972, 94–126).

On the other hand, one could interpret Harris's discussion of Washington as actually defining an ironic tone for his narrative. Folklorist Frederick L. McElroy has argued that Washington's narratives such as *Up from Slavery* appear to promote subservience and acceptance of a degraded social status without question. Yet McElroy traces in the text aspects of "vernacular black culture" and "oral traditions" that were connected to a history of struggle and survival among slaves. Within this context, texts such as Washington's *Up from Slavery* served as a clever strategic tool, providing whites with a comforting narrative that played to their racial beliefs and fears and providing African Americans with a narrative that could be understood "in the mythical context of the trickster," in which Washington was a hero superior in character and wit to whites (McElroy 1992, 92). As McElroy puts it, to many African Americans during the first half of the twentieth century,

> Washington, and other accommodationist black leaders who flourished in the pre–Civil Rights South taught as their strategy for success: to rise in America it might be necessary for a black striver to master the abstruse art of "hitting a straight lick with a crooked stick." To [many] Washington was a hero and role model. He had built a power base by developing his version of the old slave strategy of hiding aggressive intentions behind a mask of fawning servility. He had stooped to conquer. (92)[11]

If McElroy is correct, then Washington adopted an ironic stance in his narratives, forging alliances in the interest of African American struggle by appearing conciliatory and subservient to white power.[12] And Harris constructs an equally ironic narrative in which he is able to resist identification with whiteness during a time of intense hatred toward blacks by embracing African American institutions like Hampton and heroes like Washington. Harris's narrative, particularly in the way that he evokes sports, suggests that beneath the surface, Native Americans and African Americans shared common interests at a particular moment of danger in relation to racial politics. Harris further reinforces this in his memories of life at Hampton.

In the interview, he informs his questioners that Hampton was a school for African Americans but that the federal government had provided funds for Native Americans to attend the institution. Harris also reports that in 1912 Congress refused to fund appropriations for Native Americans to attend Hampton. He states that "some Indian senator came there, saw the Indians mixed with the Negroes, he was afraid that they was going to intermarry with the Negroes so he, so he went back to, to Washington, he abolished the appropriation." He is only able to remember that the senator was a "Choctaw Indian" from Oklahoma. Harris's recollections were mostly accurate. In 1912, after Democrats had gained control of the sixty-second Congress, Hampton lost the support it had had in Washington for funding. Perhaps the most powerful argument on the floor of Congress came from Democratic Representative Charles D. Carter, a member of the Chickasaw (rather than Choctaw) tribe from Oklahoma. Rather than basing his argument on intermarrying, Carter focused on what he described as the indignity of being associated with African Americans. First he pointed out that whites and blacks in Virginia were segregated in their schooling. Then he recounted the numerous allowances Indians had been forced to make over their history, concluding that "he has nothing left but his self-respect. . . . You come to him with the Hampton school and ask him to surrender his self-respect by placing his children on a social equality with an inferior race, a level to which you yourself will not deign to descend" (Lindsey 1995, 253).

It would have been easier after this happened for Harris to have left Hampton and gone to a place like Carlisle. If he had done so, he would have had the financial support of the federal government to pay for his schooling. Even more to the point, he could have followed the lead of someone like Charles Carter, attempting to gain social advancement by embracing the potential privileges of whiteness and, in turn, accepting a racial polarity in which its opposite, blackness, is associated with degradation. In fact, as Lonna Malmsheimer has argued in her analysis of the photographs taken of students at Carlisle, that the school's founders very much associated assimilation with whiteness, both in the adoption of cultural norms and in the actual, physical transformation of skin color (Malmsheimer 1987). Yet instead of going this route, Harris says that he chose to stay at Hampton, where, like Booker T. Washington before him, he proved his worthiness by working: "I cleaned the rooms, then what little I make in the shop helped me out." In fact, earlier in the interview, he put down the education at Carlisle (where a "Mexican" friend was attending after tricking the government into believing that he was an "Indian"), stating, "Ours at Hampton was higher."

In both his identification with Hampton after the loss of appropriations and in his critical memory of Carlisle, Harris conveys an irony that is similar to the one he begins with in his story about the Jack Johnson prize fight. In each case, he responds to a force pressuring him to accept white supremacy by renewing his commitment to Hampton. In addition, his story about Carlisle ironically mocks white society's arbitrary racial categories either by noting how they were subverted (by his "Mexican" friend) or by stating that the school itself failed to adequately serve Native Americans. And in his decision to stay at Hampton, he chooses to defy terms of success based upon identification with "whiteness," siding his own more ambiguous racial identity with "blackness."

Harris's narrative continues to operate in dialogue with African American culture and history in the last of his stories that I have chosen to include in this chapter. In it, he discusses how he traveled during the summer with the Hampton choir as they sang before white audiences, who would then donate money to the school. He remembers that they made a lot of money for Hampton on these tours, and that a "[l]ot of the white people take to their singing." McElroy notes that spirituals were an important category of black vernacular culture in Booker T. Washington's writing and that Washington drew upon them to manipulate whites into providing funds for his school, Tuskegee Institute. He writes that "Washington recognized how the 'old time songs' warmed the hearts of affluent whites. He sent North fund-raising quartets similar to the Fisk

Jubilee Singers, and he insisted that Tuskegee's students sing spirituals in the programs produced for the entertainment of the school's rich guests" (McElroy 1992, 93). In fact, Harris remembers on his tours with the Hampton choir that donors "always mention Booker T. Washington, where Booker T. Washington went to school."

If, as McElroy argues, this deployment of African American spirituals served as a tool of the trickster, then Harris might be seen as drawing from the particular experiences of his own Native American/Yavapai history. He reports giving speeches about American Indians and about his own tribe at these events. In addition, he would dress in the costume of the "Indian" that his white audience would recognize—"a blouse here, a waist that hangs over like the Indians wear, you know"—and perform a dance that he knew white audiences would enjoy. In his telling of the story, however, he makes it very clear at the end that he was tricking these patrons, stating, "sometimes I, I pretend I know how to dance."

Deloria notes how such performances were sometimes a component of white fascination with Native American athletics. He writes, "Like the Globetrotters, who fused athletic exhibition with a familiar minstrelsy tradition, Indian athletes were expected to display White cultural understandings of 'Indianness' to their predominantly White audiences" (Deloria 1996, 333). For example, football players on the barnstorming professional football team known as the Oorang Indians, which included Carlisle graduates Jim Thorpe and Jim Guyun, would perform a wild west halftime show, wearing war bonnets, feathers, and other "Indian" costumes for the enjoyment of white audiences. He quotes one former player as saying, "'Many of the players saw exhibition football in the same light as a touring wild west show—a chance to make some money and to have some fun.'" Deloria goes on:

> If athletics meant different things to Indians and non-Indians, then, there were also significant points of overlap, such as Indians winning "Indianness" or taking the assimilatory step toward college. Sports served as a meeting place for transformation and persistence; for distinct, even mutually exclusive Indian and White interpretations, and for shared understandings. (333)

Deloria argues that activities like sports allowed many Indians to "move more confidently in non-Indian society." After four years at Hampton, Harris certainly seemed to do this. He graduated with a degree that he remembers as being the equivalent of the completion of a freshmen year in college, then went to "Springfield YMCA College" in Massachusetts, where he trained in the counseling of young boys, and finally returned to the Yavapai reservation, where he worked in an assay office. Of course, wild west shows and minstrel performances have provided some of the most damaging and demeaning images that Native Americans and African Americans have had to live with in the United States since the middle to late nineteenth century. In fact, Harris's story is not one of either pure resistance or pure accommodation. For Native Americans and other marginalized groups, interaction with dominant society involves complex negotiations and can be extremely dangerous.

However, movement into dominant society can also bring groups like African Americans and Native Americans into contact and can provide opportunities for intellectual and social exchange. Harris constructs a narrative in which he was able to do this, one that can be read as drawing from the critical perspectives of African American history to ironically reframe his own. Just as in much of the published Native American autobiographical literature, references to popular culture and athletics form only a small part of this story. But his statements and allusions to sports and leisure are crucial, for they connect his story to "hidden transcripts," transcripts that can be read as building a powerful critique of race and racism in the United States from the multiple social locations that Harris has occupied: as a Yavapai who was brutally displaced and as a Native American who played sports, identified with blacks, and became educated into white society.

# Conclusion

In June 1993 the Associated Press in newspapers around the nation (e.g., "Garagiola Bats .400 with Tribe's Children," in the *Arizona Republic*) reported that Joe Garagiola had become the savior of baseball on the Zuni Pueblo in western New Mexico. After hearing that the Zunis had almost no equipment for their kids' baseball teams, the former major league catcher and broadcaster swept into action, collecting donations, purchasing equipment, and personally delivering it to the reservation about sixty miles south-southwest of Gallup, a place that Garagiola described as "not exactly the crossroads of the world." Garagiola was also able to secure funds to build a volleyball and basketball facility and to repair the baseball fields. In addition, he bargained with the Pennington School, a prep school in New Jersey, to offer two scholarships to Zuni students who could come east to get an education. Garagiola reported that one of the students told him, "'If I want to do and learn what I want to, I have to get off the reservation. Then I can come back and help my people.'"

Two years earlier, *Sports Illustrated* published a feature story by Gary Smith on basketball among the Crow tribe in southern Montana. The article's title was "Shadow of a Nation"; the caption beneath the title stated, "The Crows, once proud warriors, now seek glory—but often find tragedy—in basketball." The story begins with an epigraph from Plenty Coups, chief of the Crows in 1930, who is quoted as remembering,

"When the buffalo went away the hearts of my people fell to the ground, and they could not lift them up again. After this nothing happened. There was little singing anywhere." The *Sports Illustrated* article tells of basketball's popularity among the Crows and recounts the tragic fate of several star players who either died in drunken-driving accidents or dropped out of school only to face a life of menial labor and anonymity. The article notes that in spite of grinding poverty and a reservation economy in which 75 percent of the people were unemployed at the time of the article, the Crow were such fanatics about basketball that their schools had won ten Class A, B, and C championships between 1980 and 1990. Calling the Crow "the tribe that loved basketball too much," Smith interprets their enthusiasm for the game as a tragic, and even unhealthy, revival of a long-dead warrior culture:

> Of all the perplexing games that the white man had brought with him—frantic races for diplomas and dollar bills and development—here was the one that the lean, quick men on the reservations could *instinctively* play. Here was a way to bring pride back to their hollow chests and vacant eyes, some physical means, at least, for poor and undereducated men to re-attain the status they once had gained through hunting and battle. Crow men had never taken up the craftwork, weaving or metallurgy that males in other tribes had. They were warriors, meat eaters, nomads whose prestige and self esteem had come almost entirely from fulfilling an intricate set of requirements—called "counting coup"—while capturing enemy horses or waging battle. (Smith 1991, 64; emphasis added)

The *Los Angeles Times* ran a feature in the fall of 1993 on the sports program at the Sherman Indian School in Riverside, California, one of the few federally operated boarding schools for Native Americans that still is operating (Witherspoon 1993). The article portrays sports as a morally uplifting experience for students ("winning is secondary to building self worth at Sherman Indian High") who have come to Sherman "with troubled pasts or to escape *perceived* prejudice in public schools [emphasis added]." The article begins with the story of a student who seemed to have found direction in life through athletics:

One Mohave girl's problems began when she was 6. Her father died and her mother turned to alcohol. Five years later, she too, was drinking. The girl, now 16, is in her third year at Sherman Indian and plays on the girls' volleyball and basketball teams. "It keeps me going," she said about sports. "It's something to do besides just go find trouble."

On February 5, 1995, the *Albuquerque Journal* ran a front-page feature on high school basketball star Jarvis Mullahon from Navajo, New Mexico, on the Navajo reservation (McAfee 1995). The article tells of Jarvis's older brother, Shawn Ray, mentoring him into a basketball player: "Taught him to stay away from drugs and alcohol. Taught him to stay in school. Taught him to work harder, aim higher." Then it goes on to report that Shawn Ray himself was a high school dropout who ended up being hit by a pickup truck and killed while walking along the side of Interstate 40, "thought by police to be under the influence of alcohol," during the summer between Jarvis's sophomore and junior years of high school.

The death of his brother, it continues, ignited a fire in Jarvis, who ended up leading a losing Navajo Pines High School basketball team into the state tournament for the first time in its history. The team, the article states, had "brought light to the dying New Mexico town" of Navajo, a planned community built in 1960 as a mill town for the Navajo Forest Products Industry forty-five miles northwest of Gallup. According to the report, at its peak the mill employed 500 Navajos. But in 1994, "criticized for excessive cutting and financial mismanagement," the mill closed, raising the unemployment rate in the town from 17.6 percent to 66.6 percent. The article presents Jarvis as a redemptive symbol from a hopeless community: "Jarvis' exploits on the court help the People forget some of the town's problems: alcoholism, drug abuse, gang activity, vandalism."

As I write about this topic at the end of the millennium, I have come to recognize how contemporary popular narratives about Native American athletes and athletics, such as those distributed through newspapers, wire services, and popular magazines, often sound much as they did at the beginning of the century. The Garagiola story, the profile of Jarvis Mullahon, and the article on the Sherman Indian School espouse the same hopes Richard Henry Pratt had when he proposed to build a new gymnasium on the Carlisle campus: the hope that sports would uplift the race, build character, and even provide access to boarding school away from the alleged corruptions of reservation life. On the other end of the spectrum, the *Sports Illustrated* piece, like the clergy members who objected to Pratt's use of football or like BIA officials who attempted to curtail athletic functions at boarding schools, suggests that highly competitive sports can be a corrupting influence upon Native American life.

All of these narratives share some common assumptions, however, about Native American culture and history. In each case, problems on contemporary reservations are framed not as the outcome of historical events or political interests and power but as cultural deficiencies of Native Americans. Each story alludes to or directly mentions problems on reservations such as poverty, unemployment, or alcoholism. However, the articles also frame these problems outside of any social or historical contexts, making it appear that Native Americans alone are responsible for these conditions, as they are portrayed as lacking ambition, intellect, or strength of character. In each case, Native American cultures are portrayed as mired in a history of declension and death, either irrelevant and inept at dealing with modern institutions and social realities or tied to the traditions of a past that, however tragically, will never return. In the case of the *Sports Illustrated* article, such traditions are not even really cultural; instead, they are portrayed as being a product of nature. Native Americans were good at and enjoyed the game because it was one that they could "instinctively play."

Such narratives provide an easy frame of reference for learning about the history of sports at boarding schools. They are, however disturbing, comforting stories for white Americans, for they do not challenge dominant conventions in any way. Such narratives are not only about sports. They are also about dominant society and the way it deals with the legacy of imperialism and conquest. They allow most readers to feel satisfied with their society—to feel proud of its ability to take care of and help those less fortunate. Prejudice, as portrayed in the Sherman Indian School article, is only something perceived by native youths in trouble, like a crutch used to evade responsibility, rather than a social reality that limits opportunities for Native Americans. Poverty and unemployment, as addressed in the Jarvis Mullahon article, are the outcome of corruption and mismanagement by Navajo businesses rather than the outcome of federal corruption and land swindles that have benefited white-owned enterprises at the expense of Native American communities. Readers might experience sadness over what has been lost in the tragic past, and they might even feel a nostalgic or romantic longing for pre-Western civilization, but they do not have to think about any connection to, benefit from, or responsibility for that loss themselves.

I suggest that these are neither the best nor the most useful ways to think about the history of indigenous people for someone interested in learning about the lives and struggles of Native Americans or about addressing contemporary issues of relevance to Native Americans. Nor do they provide an adequate frame of reference for thinking about Native American or boarding school sports. Athletics are like any other cultural activity, far too complex and too interesting to be tied to any single set of stories. It is very important to listen to the voices of people like Arthur Harris or Jeff McCloud or the boxers, football players, and various other graduates of Carlisle, Chilocco, Flandreau, Pipestone, and Sante Fe Indian Schools. Through them, the pleasures of something like a baseball game or a boxing match are connected to stories that do not necessarily conform with those of progress or despair that nonnative people already know. Stories about boarding school sports evoke multiple histories and understandings of the past and present.

In January 1995 I attended a girls' basketball game at the Santa Fe Indian School and saw firsthand the diverse representations and experiences that are a part of Native American sports. Although Santa Fe was at one time a boarding school operated in the regimented fashion of Carlisle, it had closed as a boarding school in 1962 and reopened in 1981 under the leadership of the All Indian Pueblo Council (a body comprised of the governors of the nineteen New Mexico Pueblos). Unlike its earliest incarnation, it was now concerned with maintaining Native American life and culture as a core part of its educational mission (Hyer 1990). Just like the school itself, the game provided a vivid illustration of how sports at boarding schools continue to be meaningful on a variety of levels and in ways that are in dialogue with multiple histories.

Santa Fe's gymnasium was about half full for that night's game against Taos High School, a bigger public school that had a reputation as a perennial state power. Students almost entirely filled the second-tier bleachers. Their clothes were a far cry from those of the days of military uniforms: They wore oversized sport jackets, NBA jerseys, jeans, and sweatshirts. Parents and adult friends sat in the tier below, and students mingled at halftime catching up on developments and news about relatives at home. During the National Anthem, the fans shouted at the end "home of the BRAVES!" Ironically, Santa Fe Indian School had the same team nickname that in the context of Atlanta's Turner Field and the "tomahawk chop" is an offensive racial slur. Within the context of the school, however, students, parents, and members of the Native American communities in the region had appropriated it as a symbol of pride and team spirit.

In fact, a wooden plaque on the wall of the gym read in bold letters, "Santa Fe Indian School—Home of the Braves—Established 1890." It was but one sign in the gymnasium itself that exhibited multiple readings of sports and culture at the school. A banner representing the New Mexico Athletic Association hung at one end of the gym, pronouncing as its mission of "teaching morals, character, and the American system of achievement." At the other end hung a large mural in two parts. One represents a Navajo life, picturing a man herding sheep against a background of red desert rocks, and the other represents Pueblo traditions, picturing a dance in front of adobe pueblo architecture. The American flag is not alone on the wall, as it is accompanied by those representing the school, tribal affiliation, and the state of New Mexico. No single banner or image defined the event. Each tied the game to a strand of history to which boarding school and sports is connected.

Just as Pipestone students remembered doing during the 1930s, many at this game seemed to have come to meet and sit with members of the opposite sex or in single-sex peer groups. Couples cuddled, while friends laughed, chatted, and ate junk food as they shouted encouragement to their team. Unfortunately, the Lady Braves needed a lot of encouragement in the first half, quickly falling behind by 16, and trailing by a score of 20–30 at the half. Many students gave up on their team at that point and chose to leave the arena. However, the players on the court refused to concede, moving to within 4 points with 3:39 left in the third quarter. By the end of the period, Taos was back up by 9, but Santa Fe charged back, tying the game at the 4:59 mark in the final quarter. The gym was filled with noise as Taos went into the final minute with a 1-point lead. The Lady Braves tied it again at 52 with forty-five seconds to go, but it was not enough, and they ended up a basket short, 52–54.

A coach for the Santa Fe Indian School the next day told me that the game was a "moral victory," especially considering that the girls had just returned from Christmas break and had not had very much time to practice. Sports have an ability to present, at least ideologically, the image of a level playing field that can provide opportunities for "moral victories." As Jeff McCloud states—quoted in the epigraph of chapter 3—the opportunity to win at a fair fight might help some Native Americans to understand that bigger social losses came about as the result of battles that were not fair; in other words, to understand the present not as the result of progress or of natural forces that could not have been reversed but as the product of historical forces and of real choices. Through their athletic contests, boarding school students, and Native Americans more generally, celebrated a popular nationalism that showed "what an Indian can do." Listening and learning about the pasts to which such memories are connected is a good first step toward understanding that problems like poverty and unemployment on reservations grew out of historical circumstances that have benefited nonnative citizens at the expense of Native Americans, and not out of deficiencies of Indian culture. Such a reading of Native American athletics does not just account for the pleasure that many Native Americans have received from participating in sports; it also reveals experiences and histories that are relevant and alive in the present.

# Notes

## Introduction

1. For examples of such texts, see Oxendine 1988 and Newcombe 1975.

2. See Adams 1995; Ahern 1983; Child 1993; Coleman 1993; Ellis 1996; Hultgren and Molin 1989; Hyer 1990; Lindsey 1995; Lomawaima 1993 and 1994; Malmsheimer 1987; McBeth 1984; Szasz 1977; Trennart 1988.

## 1. Native American Athletics and Assimilation

1. For a discussion of white desire embodied in the minstrel stage, see Lott 1993.

2. I also do not want to fail to mention the degree to which this passage reveals a fundamental belief in a level of racial separation. Even though he argued that character qualities that many associate with the "white race" are shared by Indians, he assumed that the virtues, like courage, of those he encountered were racially based.

3. Wald is citing her own 1984 work "Of mimicry and Men: The Ambivalence of Discourse," in which she quotes Homi K. Bhabha.

4. See the testimony of Gus Welch before Congress in 1914 (U.S. Congress 1914). Warner's tactics are also recounted in Jack Newcombe's biography of Jim Thorpe (Newcombe 1975; Oxendine 1988, 189).

## 2. The Struggle over the Meaning of Sports

1. Although Carlisle was committed to erasing all traits of Native American identity and culture, Warner self-consciously drew from the tradition of

distance running among the Hopi when Louis Tewanima joined the track team. Tewanima not only competed successfully at Carlisle, but he finished ninth in a field of fifty-six in the 1908 London Olympics and eventually won the silver medal in the Olympic 5,000- and 10,000-meter races in 1912 (Nabokov 1981, 179–82).

## 3. The 1930s and Pan-Indian Pride

1. For this interpretation of nationalism, I draw greatly from George Lipsitz's observation about the importance of Africa for African Americans. Discussing this in relation to popular music and the importance for African Americans of preserving African cultural forms, Lipsitz writes, "Historically, Afro-Americans have treasured African retentions in speech, music, and art both as a means of preserving collective memory about a continent where they were free and as a way of shielding themselves against the hegemony of white racism. As long as Africa existed, as long as African forms contrasted with Euro-American forms, white racism was a particular and contingent American reality, not an inevitable or necessary feature of human existence" (Lipsitz 1990, 111). I would argue that the expression of such a national memory is also important, for these very same reasons, for other groups that have faced racism and marginalization, such as Native Americans.

2. Although the BIA's intent was to eliminate boarding schools, it did not succeed. In fact, many schools' enrollments actually climbed during the Great Depression. The BIA was successful, however, in building more day schools, especially for educating younger children.

3. One of the ironies of this situation is that the age of players also made it difficult to compete on the high school level, for which many students were too old. The Oklahoma State High School Athletic Association would not accept Chilocco into its ranks until 1948, as reported in the *Indian School Journal* of February 21, 1948.

4. At the very least, BIA policies themselves during the 1930s often invited critical interpretations. In an essay in the May 15, 1933, edition of *Indians at Work*, Collier criticized "planless individualism" that guided allotment policies of the previous generation. He advocated "planned cooperative use of the land and its resources." Yet this was also placed within the context of a more general patriotic agenda. Such policies on reservations, wrote Collier, "unquestionably will blaze the way on many tracks for the vaster experiment and readjustment, now being started, which is intended to bring about a rebirth of the American people—a rebirth in spirit, even more than the rebirth of a more fairly distributed

prosperity" (Collier 1933, 3). This early statement evokes a radically egalitarian vision of social relations drawn from the historical memory of many Native American groups even as it places this vision ("more fairly distributed prosperity") as of secondary importance to the national pride that Collier hoped it would foster.

## 4. Female Physical Fitness, Sexuality, and Pleasure

1. Activities like same-sex dancing were a common form of physical education for women throughout the United States during the early part of the twentieth century, particularly in settings that stressed strict segregation. Cahn, however, notes that by the 1930s such ideas about physical education, which were drawn from a Victorian ideology based upon separate male and female spheres, had begun to disintegrate. Encouragement of female bonding diminished out of fears that it might turn girls into lesbians, and companionship between men and women was generally more encouraged. Thus, at boarding schools, strict divisions between boys and girls were also relaxed during this decade, but school officials still expressed concern over the contact that this provided (Cahn 1993, 171–80).

2. In her dissertation on the Chemawa Indian School in Oregon, Debbie Ann LaCroix reports that of sixteen women whom she interviewed, thirteen discussed sexual abuse as a part of the experience of boarding school, and eight actually reported having been abused themselves (LaCroix 1993, 327–33). For another account of an incident of sexual abuse, see *Learning the White People Way* 1991.

## 5. Narratives of Boarding School Life

1. See Clifford and Marcus 1986; Marcus and Fischer 1986; Mihesuah 1998; Rosaldo 1993.

2. We did as she said, and it was not long before we had our daughter, Catherine Ann.

3. Doris Duke Native American oral history collections exist at the Arizona State Museum at the University of Arizona, UCLA, the University of New Mexico, the University of Oklahoma, the University of Florida, the University of South Dakota, and the University of Illinois.

4. The Arthur Harris interview at the Arizona State Museum is a restricted file. Anthropologist Robert Euler owns the rights to reprint portions from interviews in that file, and he has generously allowed me to include sections of the Arthur Harris interview in this book (Harris 1967).

5. For background on the history of the Indian school at Hampton Institute, see Ahern 1983; Buffalohead and Molin 1996; Hultgren and Molin 1989; Lindsey 1995; Molin 1988.

6. The correct spelling is Jeffries.

7. In fact, not only does he recall being forced to speak English, but in his story about the scholars coming to school to study Yavapai language, he illustrates how anthropologists were capturing "dying languages" at the point of their being "killed" and how they were not only accomplices in their death but an active part of the "stealing" of language. To the researchers, the Yavapai language was not part of a community or culture; rather, it became a capital resource of anthropologists, who were building for themselves an archive of linguistic expertise. This expertise would become all the more valuable as Yavapai children were taught to learn English and to allow the language itself to vanish from active use.

8. It may not have been uncommon for children like Harris to "voluntarily" attend boarding school after being hunted by tribal police. In her published autobiography, for example, Polingaysi Qoyawayma (Elizabeth Q. White) recalls that her Hopi community resisted sending children to boarding school, hiding them from Navajos who had been hired to take them away to school. After most of her friends and her sister had been captured and taken to school, she recalls thinking, "I am not happy ... I am lonely" (Qoyawayma and Carlson 1964, 24). Like Harris, she went against her parents' wishes and joined her friends at school.

9. For her quote on hidden transcripts, Caponi-Tabery cites Kelly 1996, 189. Also see Scott 1990, 1985.

10. See Ahern 1983, 101-24; Buffalohead and Molin 1996, 59–94; Hultgren and Molin 1989; Lindsey 1995; Molin 1988, 83–98.

11. I am indebted to Amanda Kemp for first steering me toward this interpretation of *Up from Slavery*.

12. Consistent with McElroy's argument, Washington repeatedly used his experiences with Indians to argue for the moral superiority of African Americans over whites. In an October 1880 issue of the *Southern Workman*, for example, he wrote of the "magnanimous spirit shown by the colored students toward the Indians at this Institution," and he continued, "It shows that though he himself was oppressed, he has become enough enlightened to rise above mere race prejudices in doing his duty toward other men. . . . I think that the treatment the Indians have received at this Institution at the hands of the colored students is quite a rebuke to many white Institutions both North and South, especially such veneered institutions as West Point, where the sons of the so called civilized parents refused to

associate with the colored boy" (Harlan et al. 1972, 85). Washington reiterated this theme more than twenty years later in his autobiography *The Story of My Life and Work*, where he wrote, "I have often wondered if there is a white institution in this country whose students would have welcomed the incoming of more than a hundred companions of another race in the cordial way that the black students at Hampton welcomed the red ones. How often have I wanted to say to white students that they lift themselves up in proportion as they help to lift others, and that the more unfortunate the race and the lower in the scale of civilization, the more does one raise one's self by giving assistance" (Washington [1900] 1969, 49). On the one hand, these passages presume that Native Americans exist "lower in the scale of civilization" than do African Americans. Yet Washington clearly uses experiences with Native Americans at Hampton to also turn this scale on its head, explicitly arguing that the superior position that whites enjoy because of their privileged racial status is also a sign of their moral corruption and inferiority.

# Works Cited

Adams, D. W. 1995. *Education for Extinction: American Indians and the Boarding School Experience, 1875–1928.* Lawrence: University Press of Kansas.

Ahern, Wilbert H. 1983. "'The Returned Indians': Hampton Institute and Its Indian Alumni, 1879–1893." *Journal of Ethnic Studies* 10 (4): 101–24.

Albers, P. C., and W. R. James. 1986. "On the Dialectics of Ethnicity: To Be or Not To Be Santee (Sioux)." *Journal of Ethnic Studies* 4 (1): 1–27.

*Annual Report of the Board of Indian Commissioners.* 1895. Washington, D.C.: U.S. Government Printing Office.

———. 1896. Washington, D.C.: U.S. Government Printing Office.

*Annual Report for Chilocco Indian School.* 1934/35. Superintendents' Annual Narrative and Statistical Reports from Field Jurisdictions of the Bureau of Indian Affairs, 1907–1938. NARA Microfilm Publication M1011. Reel 19.

———. 1936. Superintendents' Annual Narrative and Statistical Reports from Field Jurisdictions of the Bureau of Indian Affairs, 1907–1938. NARA Microfilm Publication M1011. Reel 19.

———. 1937. Superintendents' Annual Narrative and Statistical Reports from Field Jurisdictions of the Bureau of Indian Affairs, 1907–1938. NARA Microfilm Publication M1011. Reel 19.

*Annual Report of the Commissioner of Indian Affairs to the Department of the Interior.* 1880. Washington, D.C.: U.S. Government Printing Office.

———. 1881. Washington, D.C.: U.S. Government Printing Office.

———. 1883. Washington, D.C.: U.S. Government Printing Office.

———. 1890. Washington, D.C.: U.S. Government Printing Office.

*Annual Report for the Santa Fe Indian School.* 1911. Superintendents' Annual Nar-
    rative and Statistical Reports from Field Jurisdictions of the Bureau of
    Indian Affairs, 1907–1938. NARA Microfilm Publication M1011. Reel
    127.

———. 1926. Superintendents' Annual Narrative and Statistical Reports from
    Field Jurisdictions of the Bureau of Indian Affairs, 1907–1938. NARA
    Microfilm Publication M1011. Reel 127.

Anonymous Letter. 1933. October 31. NARA, RG 75, 750 for Chilocco.

Aronowitz, Stanley. 1973. *False Promises: The Shaping of American Working Class
    Consciousness.* New York: McGraw–Hill.

Ball, Eve. 1980. *Indeh: An Apache Odyssey.* Provo, Utah: Brigham Young University
    Press.

Beatty, Willard W. 1939. Letter, April 3. NARA, RG 75, 750 for Haskell.

Bloom, John. 1996. "'Show What an Indian Can Do': Sports, Memory, and
    Ethnic Identity at Federal Indian Boarding Schools." *Journal of American
    Indian Education* 33 (3): 33–48.

Boyer, Ruth McDonald, and Narcissus Duffy Gayton. 1992. *Apache Mothers and
    Daughters.* Norman: University of Oklahoma Press.

Bradfield, Larry. 1963. "A History of Chilocco Indian School." Master's thesis,
    University of Oklahoma.

Buffalohead, W. Roger, and Paulette Fairbanks Molin. 1996. "'A Nucleus of
    Civilization': American Indian Families at Hampton Institute in the Late
    Nineteenth Century." *Journal of American Indian Education* 35 (3): 59–94.

Bureau of Indian Affairs. 1941. *Manual for the Indian School Service.* Washington,
    D.C.: U.S. Government Printing Office.

Cahn, Susan. 1993. *Coming on Strong: Gender and Sexuality in Twentieth Century
    Women's Sport.* New York: Free Press.

Caponi-Tabery, Gena Dagel. 1999. "Jump for Joy: The Jump Trope in African
    America, 1937–1941." *Prospects* 24 (1): 521–74.

Cata, Juanita. 1968. Interview, September 23, 1968. *Doris Duke Oral History
    Collection,* University of New Mexico. Tape #44.

Child, Brenda. 1993. "A Bitter Lesson: Native Americans and the Government
    Boarding School Experience, 1880–1940." Ph.D. diss., University of Iowa.

Churchill, Ward, Norbert S. Hill, and Mary Jo Barlow. 1979. "An Historical
    Overview of Twentieth Century Native American Athletics." *The Indian
    Historian* 12 (4): 22–32.

Clifford, James, and George E. Marcus. 1986. *Writing Culture: The Poetics and Politics of Ethnography.* Berkeley and Los Angeles: University of California Press.

Coleman, Michael C. 1993. *American Indian Children at School, 1850–1930.* Jackson: University Press of Mississippi.

Collier, John. 1933. "At the Close of Ten Weeks." *Indians at Work,* September 15, 1–5.

Collier, John. 1935. Letter, April 5. NARA RG 75, 750 for Chilocco.

Deloria, Philip. 1996. "'I am of the Body': Thoughts on My Grandfather, Culture, and Sports." *South Atlantic Quarterly* 95 (2): 321–38.

Deloria, Vine Jr. 1969. *Custer Died for Your Sins: An Indian Manifesto.* New York: Macmillan.

Ehrenreich, Barbara, and Deirdre English. 1989. *For Her Own Good: 150 Years of the Experts' Advice to Women.* New York: Anchor Books.

Ellis, Clyde. 1996. *To Change Them Forever: Indian Education at the Rainy Mountain Boarding School, 1893–1920.* Norman: University of Oklahoma Press.

*An Enquiry into the Status of Athletics and Physical Education: Albuquerque Indian School.* 1931. NARA, RG 75, Box no. 51248–1931–750.

Fire/Lame Deer, John, and Richard Erdoes. 1972. *Lame Deer: Seeker of Visions.* New York: Simon and Schuster.

*First One Hundred Years Oral History Project (Santa Fe Indian School).* 1986–87.

Fischer, Michael. 1985. "Ethnicity and the Post-modern Arts of Memory." In James Clifford and George Marcus, eds., *Writing Culture,* 194–233. Berkeley and Los Angeles: University of California Press.

Foard, F., and W. Beatty. 1948. "Boxing Not an Approved Sport." *Indian Education* 171 (15 November): 1.

Foley, Douglas. 1990. *Learning Capitalist Culture: Deep in the Heart of Tejas.* Philadelphia: University of Pennsylvania Press.

Foucault, Michel. 1979. *Discipline and Punish: The Birth of Prison.* Translated by A. Sheridan. New York: Vintage Books.

Gorn, Elliott. 1986. *The Manly Art: Bare Knuckle Prize Fighting in America.* Ithaca, N.Y.: Cornell University Press.

Gorn, Elliot, and Warren Goldstein. 1993. *A Brief History of American Sports.* New York: Hill and Wang.

Harlan, Louis R., et al., eds. 1972. *The Booker T. Washington Papers.* Vol. 2: 1860–1889. Chicago: University of Illinois Press.

Harris, Arthur. 1967. Interview, October 2. *Euler-Yavapai Oral History Project*, Part 1: *Doris Duke Oral History Collection*. Arizona State Museum. University of Arizona. A-80.

Higham, John. 1984. *Send These to Me: Jews and Other Immigrants in Urban America*. Baltimore: Johns Hopkins University Press.

Hinton, Leanne, and Lucille J. Watahomigie, eds. 1984. *Spirit Mountain: An Anthology of Yuman Story and Song*. Tucson: Sun Tracks and University of Arizona Press.

Hoxie, Frederick. 1984. *A Final Promise: The Campaign to Assimilate the Indians, 1880–1920*. Lincoln: University of Nebraska Press.

Hultgren, Mary Lou, and Paulette Fairbanks Molin. 1989. *To Lead and To Serve: American Indian Education at Hampton Institute, 1878–1923*. Virginia Beach: Virginia Foundation for the Humanities.

Hyer, Sally. 1990. *One House, One Voice, One Heart: Native American Education at the Santa Fe Indian School*. Santa Fe: Museum of New Mexico Press.

*Indian Leader: Haskell Celebration Official Program*. 1926. 27–30 October. The Kansas Collection. University of Kansas Libraries, Lawrence.

*Information Bulletin (Haskell)*. 1940/41. Kansas Collection, University of Kansas Library.

Kelly, Robin D. G. 1997. "'We Are Not What We Seem': Rethinking Black Working-Class Opposition in the Jim Crow South." In Kenneth W. Goings and Raymond A. Mohl, eds., *The New African American Urban History*. Thousand Oaks, Calif.: Sage Publications.

LaCroix, Debbie Ann. 1993. "Indian Boarding School Daughters Coming Home: Survival Stories as Oral Histories of Native American Women." Ph.D. diss., University of Oregon.

Larner, J. W., ed. 1983. *The Papers of Carlos Montezuma* (microfilm). Wilmington, Del.: Scholarly Resources.

*Learning the White People Way: A Documentary Essay on the History of Federal Indian Boarding Schools*. 1991. Produced by Steven Smith and Ted Mato. Minnesota Public Radio, local station KSJN, St. Paul, Minnesota. Rebroadcast April 21, 1997.

Lindsey, Donal F. 1995. *Indians at Hampton Institute, 1877–1923*. Urbana and Chicago: University of Illinois Press.

Lipsitz, George. 1990. *Time Passages: Collective Memory and American Popular Culture*. Minneapolis: University of Minnesota Press.

Littlefield, Alice. 1989. "The BIA Boarding School: Theories of Resistance and Social Reproduction." *Humanity and Society* 13 (4): 428–41.

Lomawaima, K. Tsianina. 1993. "Domesticity in the Federal Indian Schools: The Power of Authority over Mind and Body." *American Ethnologist* 20 (2): 227–40.

———. 1994. *They Called It Prairie Light: The Story of Chilocco Indian School.* Lincoln: University of Nebraska Press.

Lott, Eric. 1993. "White Like Me: Racial Cross-Dressing and the Construction of American Whiteness." In Amy Kaplan and Donald E. Pease, eds., *The Cultures of United States Imperialism*, 474–95. Durham, N.C.: Duke University Press.

Malmsheimer, Lonna. 1985. "'Imitation White Man': Images of Transformation at the Carlisle Indian School." *Studies in Visual Communication* 11 (4): 54–75.

———. 1987. "Photographic Analysis as Ethnohistory: Interpretive Strategies." *Visual Anthropology* 1: 21–36.

Marcus, George E., and Michael M. J. Fischer. 1986. *Anthropology as Cultural Critique: An Experimental Moment in the Human Sciences.* Chicago: University of Chicago Press.

McAfee, Sean. 1995. "Navajo's Best Shot." *Albuquerque Journal.* February 5.

McBeth, Sally. 1984. *Ethnic Identity and the Boarding School Experience of West-Central Oklahoma American Indians.* New York: University Press of America.

McDonald, F. W. 1931. Letter, November 11. NARA RG 75, 750 for Haskell.

McElroy, Frederick L. 1992. "Booker T. Washington as Literary Trickster." *Southern Folklore* 49 (2): 89–107.

Meriam, Lewis, et al. 1928. *The Problem of Indian Administration.* Washington, DC: Brookings Institute.

Mihesuah, Devon, ed. 1998. *Natives and Academics: Researching and Writing about American Indians.* Lincoln: University of Nebraska Press.

Miller, Dan, and David Wenner. 1997. "Thorpe's Daughter Seeks New Honor for Dad." *The Carlisle (Pennsylvania) Sentinal*, October 20.

Molin, Paulette Fairbanks. 1988. "'Training the Hand, the Head, and the Heart': Indian Education at Hampton Institute." *Minnesota History*, fall: 83–98.

Montezuma, Carlos. 1907. "Carlisle's Athletic Policy Criticized by Dr. Montezuma." *Chicago Sunday Tribune*, November 24.

Mossman, E. D. 1926. Letter to the Commissioner of Indian Affairs, September 14. National Archives, RG 75, Box no. 2380–24–750.

Nabokov, Peter. 1981. *Indian Running: Native American History and Tradition*. Santa Fe, N.M.: Ancient City Press.

Newcombe, Jack. 1975. *The Best of the Athletic Boys: The White Man's Impact on Jim Thorpe*. New York: Doubleday.

Novak, Michael. 1976. *The Joy of Sports*. New York: Basic Books.

One of Them. 1914. "The Temptations of an Athlete." *The Red Man*, June, 438–40.

Oriard, Michael. 1993. *Reading Football: How the Popular Press Created an American Spectacle*. Chapel Hill: University of North Carolina Press.

Oxendine, Joseph B. 1988. *American Indian Sports Heritage*. Champaign, Ill.: Human Kinetics Books.

Peairs, H. B. 1926. Letter to Rev. Harry Treat, November 12. National Archives, RG 75, Box no. 2380–24–750.

Pratt, Richard Henry. Native American History and Culture: Papers of Richard Henry Pratt. Yale University, Beinecke Library, Collection of Western Americana.

———. 1964. *Battlefield and Classroom: Four Decades with the American Indian, 1867–1904*. Edited by Robert M. Utley. New Haven, Conn.: Yale University Press.

Putney, Dianet. 1980. "Fighting the Scourge: American Indian Morbidity and Federal Policy, 1897–1928." Ph.D. diss., Marquette University.

Qoyawayma, Polingaysi (Elizabeth Q. White), and Vada F. Carlson. 1964. *No Turning Back: A Hopi Indian Woman's Struggle To Live in Two Worlds*. Albuquerque: University of New Mexico Press.

Rawick, George. 1972. *From Sundown to Sunup: The Making of the Black Community*. Westport, Conn.: Greenwood Press.

Reel, Estelle. 1901. *Uniform Course of Study*. Washington, D.C.: U.S. Government Printing Office.

Resolution from the Annual Conference of Indian Missionary Workers. 1926. Anadarko, Oklahoma, October 19–20. National Archives, RG 75, Box no. 2380–24–750.

Reyna, D., and Santa Fe Indian School students (producer and director). 1987. *Santa Fe Indian School: A Remembrance*. Film. Available from the Santa Fe Indian School, 1501 Cerrillos Rd., Santa Fe, New Mexico, 87502.

Roediger, David. 1991. *The Wages of Whiteness: Race and the Making of the American Working Class*. New York: Verso.

Rosaldo, Renato. 1993. *Culture and Truth: The Remaking of Social Analysis.* 2nd ed. Boston: Beacon Press.

Ryan, Carmelita S. 1962. "The Carlisle Indian Industrial School." Ph.D. diss., Georgetown University.

Sammons, Jeffrey. 1988. *Beyond the Ring: The Role of Boxing in American Society.* Urbana and Chicago: University of Illinois Press.

Schultz, April R. 1991. "'The Pride of the Race Had Been Touched': The 1925 Norse-American Immigration Centennial and Ethnic Identity." *Journal of American History* 77 (4): 1265–95.

———. 1994. *Ethnicity on Parade: Inventing the Norwegian American through Celebration.* Amherst: University of Massachusetts Press.

Scott, James C. 1985. *Weapons of the Weak: Everyday Forms of Peasant Resistance.* New Haven, Conn.: Yale University Press.

———. 1990. *Domination and the Art of Resistance: Hidden Transcripts.* New Haven, Conn.: Yale University Press.

Shawnee, George. 1935. Letter, May 10. NARA, RG 75, 750 for Haskell.

Shutes, Jeanne, and Jill Mellick. 1996. *The Worlds of P'Otsunu: Geronima Cruz Montoya of San Juan Pueblo.* Albuquerque: University of New Mexico Press.

Skinner, Carl H. 1958. *Good Indians.* New York: Comet Books.

Smith, Gary. 1991. "Shadow of a Nation." *Sports Illustrated,* February 18, 60–74.

Szasz, Margaret Connell. 1977. *Education and the American Indian: The Road to Self-Determination since 1928.* Albuquerque: University of New Mexico Press.

Talayesva, Don. 1942. *Sun Chief: The Autobiography of a Hopi Indian.* Edited by Leo Simmons. New Haven: Yale University Press.

Treat, Harry H. 1926. Letter to Charles Burke, Commissioner of Indian Affairs, October 23. National Archives, RG 75, Box no. 2380–24–750.

Trennart, Robert A. 1988. *The Phoenix Indian School: Forced Assimilation in Arizona, 1891–1935.* Norman: University of Oklahoma Press.

Trimble, Stephen. 1993. *The People: Indians of the Southwest.* Santa Fe, N.M.: School of American Research Press.

U.S. Congress. 1914. *Report to Investigate Indian Affairs.* 63rd Cong. 2nd Sess.

Wald, Priscilla. 1984. "Of Mimicry and Men: The Ambivalence of Colonial Discourse." *October* 28 (spring): 125–33.

———. 1993. "Terms of Assimilation: Legislating Subjectivity in the Emerging Nation." In Amy Kaplan and Donald E. Pease, eds., *The Cultures of United States Imperialism,* 59–84. Durham, N.C.: Duke University Press.

Washington, Booker T. [1900] 1969. *The Story of My Life and Work*. Reprint. New York: Negro Universities Press.

Warner, Glenn S. 1907. Letter to J. H. Dortch. National Archives Record Group 75, file 750 for Carlisle.

———. 1931a. "The Indian Massacres." *Collier's Weekly*, October 17, 7–8, 61–63.

———. 1931b. "Heap Big Run-Most-Fast." *Collier's Weekly*, October 24, 18–19, 46.

———. 1931c. "Red Menaces." *Collier's Weekly*, October 31, 16–17, 51.

Witherspoon, Wendy. 1993. "Taken to Heart." *Los Angeles Times*, November 9.

Witmer, Linda. 1993. *The Indian Industrial School: Carlisle, Pennsylvania, 1879–1918*. Carlisle, Pa.: Cumberland County Historical Society.

# Index

**John Bloom** is author of *A House of Cards: Baseball Card Collecting and Popular Culture* (Minnesota, 1997).